UNDIPLOMATIC NOTES

UNDIPLOMATIC NOTES

Tales from the Canadian Foreign Service

Sidney Freifeld

Illustrations by Susan Macartney

HOUNSLOW

To the memory of my dear wife Crenia
and to my daughters, Riva and Miriam

Undiplomatic Notes
Tales from the Canadian Foreign Service

Second Printing, November 1990

Copyright © 1990 by Sidney A. Freifeld
All Rights Reserved

ISBN-0-88882-126-3

Publisher: Anthony Hawke
Editor: Dennis Mills
Designer: Gerard Williams
Composition: Accurate Typesetting Ltd.
Printer: Gagné Printing Ltd.
Interior Illustrations: Susan Macartney
Front Cover Illustration: Gerard Williams

Publication was assisted by the Canada Council and
the Ontario Arts Council.

Hounslow Press
A Division of Anthony R. Hawke Limited
124 Parkview Avenue,
Willowdale, Ontario, Canada M2N 3Y5

Printed and bound in Canada

Contents

Preface

When chatting with former colleagues from the Canadian foreign service, I have found that our conversation is not likely to dwell on the sagacity of the reports we sent to the Department of External Affairs in Ottawa from our embassies abroad, or on the brilliant negotiating coups we scored against wily foreign adversaries. Rather, we often exchange stories about the amusing and even ludicrous situations in which we sometimes found ourselves while serving the movers and shakers on the world's stage.

Indeed, conversation seems to take the same turn when I meet up with diplomatic colleagues from other countries. There seems to be an element of universality, a sort of common denominator, in our lives and work. This derives, perhaps, from continuing exposure to national and world figures. Not surprisingly, we may find them somewhat more fallible than they would like their publics to believe. They may have chinks in their armour which we can detect from close range. They may possess foibles not dissimilar from those of more ordinary mortals.

These *Tales from the Canadian Foreign Service* are mostly vignettes from the life of a Canadian diplomatic officer, and focus on the odd and sometimes bizarre experiences that

1

helped to enliven my years with the Department of External Affairs. While my own career happened to be in the Canadian foreign service, what I relate in the tales could equally have befallen officers of the United States' Department of State, Britain's Foreign and Commonwealth Office, the French Quai d'Orsay, or the Ministries of Foreign Affairs of the Netherlands, Ireland, Australia, Norway and many other countries.

Some readers of these tales may be acquainted with Lawrence Durrell's inimitable trilogy — *Esprit de Corps, Stiff Upper Lip* and *Sauve Qui Peut* — which relate hilarious goings-on at a mythical British embassy in the Balkans after the end of World War II. Durrell did spend some time in the British foreign service, and I am, therefore, not certain how fanciful or apocryphal his stories might be. In any event I can assure my readers that the episodes I describe really did happen, just the way I have related them.

This book does not purport to analyze Canada's international relations or describe how foreign policy is formulated — an esoteric subject about which much has already been written over the years. What it does seek to do is to amuse. And, incidentally, it may answer, at least in part, questions frequently put to us by persons in less exciting but more remunerative pursuits, questions such as, "What do you really *do* in the foreign service?" or "What kind of lives do you actually lead?" Life in Canada's diplomatic corps may not be a way to grow wealthy, but there is rarely a dull moment if you can stand the gaff. And for those who survive it, it has its own rewards.

Some of these tales have been published in Toronto's *Globe and Mail* in recent years, usually under the title of "Tales from External Affairs," and several have been published in Montreal's *Gazette*. A few have appeared in *bout de papier*, a quarterly published by the Professional Association of Foreign Service Officers (our trade union). Three have been published in abridged form in the *Reader's Digest*. Others are seeing the light of day for the first time in this book.

Among the persons I wish to thank for assistance in one form or another in preparing this volume is, first and foremost, my late wife, Crenia, who shared with me the joys and vicissitudes of service for over thirty-two years — in Ottawa, New York, Mexico City, Dublin, Montevideo, Bogota and Quito. Dr Donald Page, until 1989 External's senior historian, often pointed the way to unearthing tid-bits from the Department's early files, which served as the basis for several of these tales. Debra Hulley, a member of the staff of the Professional Association of Foreign Service Officers, devoted much time, with great enthusiasm, in helping me prepare the manuscript for publication. And my thanks are owing to a number of External Affairs colleagues, both serving and — like myself — retired, whose experiences form the basis of several chapters.

New York and the United Nations

A Slip of the Tongue

Nominations for The Canadian of the Past Half Century and More would surely have to include General A.G.L. McNaughton, not only for his lofty achievements as soldier, scientist, diplomat, administrator and engineer, but also because there was a curious chink in his armour. This provided an insight into a side of his personality unsuspected by the soldiers who served under him or by the general public.

I had a chance to observe this while serving at the Canadian Mission to the United Nations in the early years after World War II, when the General was appointed Canada's first ambassador and permanent representative to the United Nations.

When General McNaughton came down to New York he already bore an awesome list of credentials. He had organized and trained the First Canadian Army during the war. He had headed the internationally prestigious National Research Council in Ottawa and served as chairman of the Canadian section of the Canada-United States Permanent Joint Board on Defence. He had also represented Canada on the United Nations Atomic Energy Commission and had, at one time, been minister of national defence and a member of Prime Minister Mackenzie King's cabinet. And much more.

As those of us at Canada's UN Mission in New York — which included George Ignatieff and John Starnes — were soon to find out, the General was a man of boundless energy. He tackled his new career of diplomacy with a high sense of dedication and enthusiasm.

His capacity for work and for homework was prodigious (none of this "keep your memos to one page" nonsense) and his resilience extraordinary. After Canada was elected to a two-year term on the Security Council, for 1948–49, his pace became gruelling, as he was deeply involved in the disputes between India and Pakistan, the Netherlands and Indonesia, the Arab world and Israel, and East and West, with the Cold War enveloping all of them.

However nothing in the General's imposing curriculum vitae had prepared us for the peculiar qualities he began to display on the podium at the United Nations — including a propensity for mispronunciations, malapropisms, gaffes and plain slips of the tongue.

As soon as the General began speaking at UN meetings he revealed a tendency for mispronouncing or garbling names which, perhaps in some obscure Freudian fashion, were associated in his mind with someone or something disagreeable. For example, he had no trouble at all with the name of Sir Alexander Cadogan, his British colleague, or Sir Zafrullah Kahn of Pakistan, whom he greatly admired. But he found Soviet Foreign Minister Vishinsky politically antagonistic and personally disagreeable, and his name invariably came out of the General's mouth as "Viskinsky" or "Visnisky." He smoothly pronounced such tongue-twisters as the New Orleans *Times-Picayune* or the *Neue Zürcher Zeitung*, if they supported some stand he had taken, but when he wanted to object to a criticism advanced by the Moscow daily *Pravda*, it came out "Pravada"; I never heard him even attempt to speak of its sister daily *Izvestia*.

When the General wanted to refer to a previous speaker

at the General Assembly's rostrum, it came out "nostrum."
He would describe some delegate's machinations or confusions as "higlady-piglady." "Façade" came out "fackaide."
He also had an ever-so-slight lisp, and when he referred
to the "*pithy* remarks" of a previous speaker, the words
that came out had a startling effect on his listeners and,
incidentally, created just the opposite effect that he had intended. All these oddities quickly became known among us
as McNaughtonisms, and they caused as much surprise
among his ambassadorial colleagues as among his juniors.
We never knew what he might come up with next. George
Ignatieff, who was then his principal adviser, in later years
advanced the thesis that the General's propensity to mispronounce may have reflected an unconscious sense of
humour.

Whatever the explanation, we were quite unprepared for
the choicest McNaughtonism of all — which fell from the
General's lips on the night of March 31, 1948.

At the beginning of that year, Canada had begun a two-
year term as a member of the Security Council, the chairmanship of which rotated monthly among the member
countries in alphabetical order. At the end of each month's
term, it was the custom for each chairman to give a private
dinner for his ambassadorial colleagues on the Council.

Canada's turn came in February and, at the end of the
month, McNaughton's dinner proved blessedly uneventful.
In March it was China's turn to preside. Cold-War tensions
had continued to mount. They fuelled unbelievably acrimonious debate in the UN's old meeting halls out in the Long
Island towns of Lake Success and Flushing, especially
between such redoubtable antagonists as Andrei Gromyko,
the dour, hard-nosed USSR representative on the Security
Council and the USA's pugnacious Senator Warren Austin, a
veteran of the wars on Capitol Hill.

In addition, Canada's own relations with the Soviet Union
had become especially sensitive, owing to the sensational
defection to the Canadian authorities of Igor Gouzenko, a

cipher clerk at the USSR's Embassy in Ottawa. His revelations
— the first of their kind in the postwar years and backed up
with numerous documents he purloined from his embassy's
code room — about the extent of Soviet espionage and
subversion in Canada and other Western nations had
shocked the USSR's erstwhile wartime allies, and had reverberated around the world.

When General McNaughton went to the Chinese ambassador's dinner on the last day of the month, he found that
Senator Austin had brought along Henry Wallace. Wallace
had been vice-president of the United States during one of
Franklin Roosevelt's terms, and in 1948 was secretary of
commerce in Harry Truman's cabinet.

Chatting after dinner with Secretary Wallace and Mr Gromyko, the General found the Russian even more dour and
gloomy than usual. Mr Gromyko complained moodily about
life in the United States and the problems of day-to-day living
in New York City (in fact his home was a sumptuous estate
on Long Island's north shore). He was finding life in New
York unbearable. Everything he ate was canned or packaged,
even apples. He simply wasn't able to find a decent, fresh,
eatable apple.

Mr Wallace, himself a mid-Western farmer and not
inclined to take this lightly, replied: "Well, you might not like
our packaging of food, but people in the United States at least
have a wider choice of food than in the Soviet Union." He
went on: "And furthermore, we have an extensive trade in
food products between the United States and Canada. Here,
if you don't like an American apple, you can often buy some
alternative from Canada."

Turning to General McNaughton, Mr Wallace continued:
"General, can you suggest some Canadian apples that Mr
Gromyko might find more acceptable at this time of year?
What are some of your favourite varieties up in Canada that
our Soviet colleague might try?"

Without hesitation, the General replied crisply: "MacIntosh *Reds* and Northern *Spies*."

The conversation, with the shadow of Igor Gouzenko hovering overhead, dropped like a lump of lead.

When the General gave his account of the dinner the next morning at the Canadian Mission he seemed preoccupied, and concerned that although his Reds and Spies blooper was quite spontaneous, he might have offended Gromyko. He wondered whether he should write a note of apology.

George Ignatieff, himself of Russian origin, suggested to the General that he might have underestimated Gromyko's sense of humour; Mr Gromyko might well have had a good laugh and regaled his own colleagues back at the USSR Mission with the story.

This satisfied the General, for the time being. Then, when he learned that Ignatieff had mentioned the episode to External Affairs Under-Secretary "Mike" Pearson on the telephone and that Mr Pearson had in turn mentioned it at a press conference, the General sternly admonished his principal adviser with: "Ignatieff, I don't like humour."

Would Your
Daughter Marry A...

To his close friends and neighbours in the early days of the United Nations, the awarding of the 1950 Nobel Peace Prize to Ralph Bunche came hardly as a surprise. We knew him not only as a wonderful human being but suspected that, within a few years, he would become one of the world's top diplomatists and an outstanding black American of his generation. Completely unpretentious, he also had a fine sense of humour — understandably tinged with a bittersweet irony when recounting the extraordinary situations in which he sometimes found himself. Very handsome, and bearing an infectious smile, Bunche, for whatever reason of genetics, was a rather light-complexioned black.

In 1950, the American Supreme Court's decision on school desegregation, the Alabama sit-ins, Martin Luther King's "We shall overcome" marches, and the whole civil rights movement were still years in the future. Student busing and affirmative action were unheard of.

After distinguished service in the wartime Office of Strategic Services and the State Department, Bunche was an early appointee to the top echelon of the United Nations Secretariat, as under-secretary for special political affairs. In this capacity he performed the remarkable achievement of negotiating armistice agreements between Israel and the Arab states that had attacked her in 1948-49. Because the Arab nations did not recognize Israel and would not meet with her representatives, Bunche was forced to perform a nimble pre-Kissinger type of shuttle diplomacy on the Island of Rhodes. It was for his success in these endeavours that he was awarded the Peace Prize and received world-wide acclaim.

At that time we were neighbours of the Bunches in Parkway Village, a 700-unit garden apartment development on Long Island that had been leased by the United Nations to house families coming in from all parts of the world — members of the UN Secretariat, of Missions to the UN, and of the international press corps. Parkway Village helped them overcome the housing shortage and special problems faced by newcomers from far-off continents. The residents had black, yellow or brown skins, boasted widely differing ethnic backgrounds, and most of them felt utterly at sea in North American day-to-day living.

My immediate neighbour and closest friend was the UN's top African expert, Heinz Wieschhoff, an anthropologist, who was later to accompany Dag Hammarskjold on the secretary-general's ill-fated trip to the Congo, where they both died in a plane crash. Wieschhoff worked closely with Bunche, and our three families were occasionally together. Mrs Bunche, Virginia Wieschhoff and my wife, Crenia, worked closely with Mrs Alva Myrdal to help the fledgling United Nations International School through its early struggling days — long before it became the famous educational institution it is today and before it began to receive support from the UN budget and from member nations. Ralph Bunche Jr, the Wieschhoff children and my daughter Riva were all friends and fellow students in the school's first class — kindergarten — and together they went through the successive grades that the school struggled to add, one by one, each year.

Our conversation would sometimes turn to the oddities

encountered in living in Parkway Village and working at the United Nations. One evening, Crenia mentioned that the neighbouring Edingers — he was Agence France Presse UN bureau chief — had sent us a handsome invitation card presenting their compliments and requesting the pleasure of our presence, but with the sole and uninformative notation "9:30 p.m. Thursday." We assumed that this was the crisp French way of saying "come around after dinner Thursday for a cup of coffee and a drop of Grand Marnier." So we ate heartily at home and were shaken to find ourselves facing an exquisite and sumptuous French dinner on arrival.

Then Ralph casually mentioned that he had been at quite a dinner himself a few nights earlier — a White Tie and Decorations affair given by UN Secretary-General Trygve Lie in honour of Crown Prince Olaf of Norway, who was visiting the United States at that time. Lie himself was a Norwegian. The Nobel Peace Prize award to Bunche had just been announced, generating world-wide publicity, and he would soon be off to Oslo to accept it.

Other guests included the visiting head of the Swedish-American Line — most people still crossed the Atlantic by ship in those days — and his American wife, next to whom Ralph found himself seated at dinner. When she asked whether he had ever been to Scandinavia, Ralph replied that he would soon be going over to Oslo.

"What are you going there for?" she asked.

"Well, it's in connection with the Nobel Peace Prize," Ralph replied.

"Oh, That Thing. Who on earth are they giving it to this year?" she wanted to know.

While Ralph was mulling over how he should reply, Trygve Lie proposed a toast to President Truman of the United States.

"Imagine having to drink to the honour of that tie sales-man in the White House!" the American lady muttered to Ralph. (At one time Truman had owned a haberdasher's shop in Kansas City.)

To this, Bunche ventured to suggest that perhaps one of the good things about the United States was that a tie sales-man *could* make it to the White House. To this she retorted: "All this nonsense about equality — why the negroes are beginning to get more and more uppity and first thing you know they'll want to be going to our schools and swimming at our beaches."

At this moment the guest on her other side got up from his chair and whispered something in Trygve Lie's ear, and he, in turn, whispered in Prince Olaf's ear.

Wanting to cool it with the lady, Ralph responded that he could understand that negroes might feel they needed good schooling and also that they might want to be able to swim at a decent beach.

But the American lady wasn't having any of it and Ralph, with *déja vue* sensation, listened to her say: "Well you know where all that's going to lead to. They'll soon be wanting to marry with our children. Now how would *you* like it if *your* daughter married a negro?"

As Ralph related it to us that evening with an ever-so-wistful grin: "While I was wondering whether I should make my stock reply in this situation — that that was probably what my daughter *will* do when she's grown up — one of Trygve Lie's aides came over and told her she was wanted in the ante-room. She got up and slipped out — and never returned to the dinner."

A Little Difficulty
With Our Language

The pitfalls that can be encountered when having to speak in a language not one's own were illustrated incisively by United Nations Secretary-General U Thant in 1968 when he addressed the annual dinner given in his honour by the UN Correspondents' Association. The secretary-general confined himself, during his speech, to illustrating only one of the vagaries of everyday English — the malapropism. He passed over such delightful oddities as gaffes, mispronunciations and slips-of-the-tongue.

The malapropism is the misuse, sometimes ludicrously, of an ordinary word; for example, when a delegate says "the speaker before me has an *incredulous* capacity for misrepresentation," or a candidate for a post in the secretariat says, "if I *reprehend* the regulations correctly, this is no place to grow rich."

By contrast the gaffe is a *gaucherie, faux pas*, blunder, blooper or boner. It would be no denigration of Canada's first ambassador to the United Nations, General A.G.L. McNaughton, to call his "MacIntosh Reds and Northern Spies" remark to Andrei Gromyko a fine example of gaffe, doubtless not committed out of ignorance. Mispronunciation, when the speaker knows and uses a word correctly but garbles it in speech, is by no means confined to the United Nations. The earliest example that comes to mind is when my mother, who emigrated to Canada from Eastern Poland, used to refer to neighbouring "Chesnoslovakia." Finally, the slip-of-the-tongue — as when Joe Clark, when he was prime minister, used to refer to the leader of the opposition as "Prime Minister Trudeau."

When U Thant accepted the UN Correspondents' Association's invitation it was a repeat performance, since he had spoken at its dinner every year since he had taken office. Furthermore, such a gathering — like its counterparts, the Gridiron Dinner in Washington, or the Parliamentary Press Gallery Annual Dinner in Ottawa — is difficult to address. Whether the speaker is the United Nations secretary-general, the president of the United States or the prime minister of Canada, he is someone his audience has covered around the clock for years. It will have heard hundreds of his speeches and jokes and will doubt whether he can have anything new to say. The ground rule is that he cannot be reported, so the press can have an evening of fun. Some of the journalists will be more concerned about putting on their own skit than in listening to another speech. The hotel ballroom will be noisy, the correspondents and their diplomatic guests will have overeaten, and they will want to dance, or swap stories with old friends, or simply hit the sack.

This is a tough audience for even the most eloquent United Nations secretary-general and especially for a laconic Burmese, speaking in a tongue not his own, and to cynics and skeptics looking for any sign of him tilting on the diplomatic tightrope that every secretary-general must walk if he is to remain *persona grata* to the diverse membership of the United Nations.

When U Thant got to his feet and launched into his opening remarks, his subject, as I recall, was the United Nations' accomplishments in the peaceful settlement of disputes. But he started off by remarking how difficult it was to address such a gathering in a language not his own. Problems of language could arise in many ways at the United Nations, he went on, and to illustrate the point he recalled when an ambassador was receiving an honorary degree at a North American university. It was Convocation Day and the chancellor of the university was about to present diplomas to graduates. The ambassador noticed that in the front section of the auditorium, reserved for families of the graduating class, sat a poorly dressed woman who appeared to be of immigrant origin. She sat enthralled as the students moved up to receive the coveted parchment and, when the chancellor presented one to her son, she was visibly overcome.

Then the university's president began his address. As he proceeded, the mother drank in every word. When he finished, she could restrain herself no longer and, rushing to the rostrum, seized him by the hand. "Mr President," she exclaimed, "I thought your speech was absolutely *superfluous!*"

The president was taken aback by this outburst. Then, as he realized the foreign accent in her speech, he kept a straight face and said: "I'm so glad you enjoyed my address. Now tell me, do you think it should be published *posthumously?*"

Without hesitating, she replied: "Absolutely, Mr President, and *the sooner the better!*"

With this introduction to the malapropism, U Thant won the hearts and minds of his cynical and hard-boiled journalistic and diplomatic audience. He then began his address on the peaceful settlement of disputes.

TV Socko
at the UN

Every time I hear another tirade about the evil and sinister pervasiveness of American cultural imperialism, I think back to some bizarre things that happened when Canada's Lorne Greene showed up in New York in 1967 and asked me to show him around the United Nations and, especially, to get him into a meeting of the Security Council.

Working at the UN gives one extraordinary proximity to, and sometimes familiarity with, many of the movers and shakers on the international stage, as well as our Canadian masters. A few months' UN exposure to sultans, beys, ayatollas, princes and presidents serves (or certainly should serve) to immunize Canadian foreign service officers — if not their visitors — from celebrity consciousness. A prominent Torontonian whom I had taken to lunch in the delegates' dining room nearly fainted when British Foreign Minister Anthony Eden, lunching at the next table with U.S. Secretary of State Dean Acheson, asked if he could borrow the salt from our table. One day Fidel Castro, clad in battle fatigues and chomping on a cigar, plopped down beside me on a couch in the delegates' lounge and, discovering that I could speak Spanish, practically put me on his lap to tell me

how much be admired Canada's enlightened policy towards
his country. The Ottawa visitor I had with me was very
impressed. (You rapidly get used to this kind of thing — or
you shouldn't be serving at Canada's Permanent Mission
to the United Nations.) Surely then, Lorne Greene, from a
totally strange planet — Hollywood and U.S. national tv —
would be incognito and incident-proof in the United
Nations' ambiance.

Lorne Greene was an Ottawa boy who had become a
famous radio correspondent and announcer during World
War II, and he had been sent by CBC to New York in the
early postwar years to study television, which had not yet
come to Canada. We had been friends in Ottawa and neighbours in the early years while he was in New York. By the
1960s, Lorne had become North America's outstanding tv
personality because of his weekly show, "Bonanza," which
he had created for an American network and in which he
starred as Ben Cartwright, the robust owner of the sprawling
Ponderosa Ranch. "Bonanza" was not only No. 1 in the
network ratings but so popular internationally that it was
dubbed or sub-titled into dozens of foreign-language ver-
sions. Lorne, walking down a street in any American town,
would have been recognized by more people than the governor of the state, possibly even more than the president of the
United States.

Lorne's visit to the UN took place in the middle of the Six
Day War in the Middle East. Canada was then a member of
the Security Council, which was meeting around the clock
seven days a week.

When Lorne arrived at the United Nations building on
First Avenue for his visit, the Security Council had been
meeting — in public and private sessions — nearly all the
previous night, coping with the Six Day War. To my surprise
I found the UN guards on First Avenue and at the UN
entrance doors asking Lorne to autograph their hats or any
piece of paper they could find in their pockets. I quickly led
him to the crowded visitors' gallery of the Security Council

chamber and placed him in an inconspicuous seat on which I had earlier placed my briefcase so as to hold it for him.

As I led him down the visitors' gallery steps to his seat, members of several delegations on the Security Council floor began pointing up at him in joyful recognition. UN Secretariat members then began to look up, recognize him and smile with delight. The normally unflappable simultaneous interpreters, each enclosed in a soundproof glass booth for the different UN official languages, gesticulated to each other and pointed to Lorne while carrying on with their rapid-fire translation of the momentous statements being made on the Security Council floor.

Delegation members began leaving their seats, walking across the chamber floor and climbing the steps of the visitors' gallery to Lorne's row, holding out their copy of that day's Security Council agenda for him to autograph. When I got down to my Canadian delegation seat on the chamber floor, members of other delegations came over to ask whether I would be bringing Lorne down to sit with us (strictly forbidden), as they too wanted autographs. The inscrutable Burmese UN secretary-general, U Thant, broke into a rare smile when an aide whispered in his ear what was causing all the commotion. Hans Tabor, the Danish permanent representative, who was Security Council chairman that day, finally rapped his gavel to bring the meeting back to order.

When I took Lorne to lunch in the overcrowded delegates' dining room, *maitre d*'s vied with each other to lead us to a choice table, doubtless previously reserved for some visiting head of state. Delegates and their guests, as well as waitresses and busboys, came over to our table with that day's luncheon menu for Lorne to sign; word must even have gotten through to the kitchens because a couple of UN cooks surfaced at our table and took off their chef's hats to be autographed. We ate splendidly. I had never received such good service in the delegates' dining room before — and I have never had it since.

After all these goings-on, I thought it wise not to take Lorne to the delegates' lounge for an espresso, and so I led him down the busy corridor leading from the lounge to the Council Chamber to put him back to the visitors' gallery for the resumption of the meeting. The Soviet ambassador and deputy permanent representative to the United Nations, Nicolai Federenko, and his dour boss, USSR Foreign Minister Andrei Gromyko, were strolling along the corridor towards us. I was Number Three at the Canadian Permanent Mission at the time and Federenko had never had the time of day for me before. But that day, with Lorne Green in tow, he greeted me effusively and, turning to Lorne, clasped him with out-stretched arms.

"My distinguished representative from Ponderosa, my dear Ambassador Cartwright from Bonanza," Federenko exclaimed to my, and to Andrei Gromyko's, astonishment. "I want you to know that for years you have been one of my own family. You are with us after dinner in our family living room in Moscow. You are with us in our family living room here in New York. You are one of our very own. You must autograph something for my children." He searched his pockets and finally pulled out a copy of that afternoon's Security Council agenda, which Lorne signed, with a few extra words, in front of the amazed Gromyko.

Before we headed off to the visitors' gallery entrance, Federenko urged Lorne to visit the Soviet Union and to be sure to let him know if he was coming to Moscow, so that he could be taken home to meet the Federenko family. I gather that Lorne subsequently did make a visit to the USSR but, as I did not see him again after that unbelievable day at the United Nations, I don't know whether he ever got in touch with Federenko and met his family.

But I do know that I have never had a more striking example of the all-encompassing, sinister, malevolent per-vasiveness of American cultural imperialism.

An MP
in Manhattan

Working abroad in the foreign service may provide unexpected compensation — a more intimate and rewarding view of members of parliament than you are likely to obtain in Ottawa.

To Externalites stationed at Canada's Permanent Mission to the United Nations, the autumnal visit by parliamentary observers generates a happy rather than a fearful prospect, for we have learned that any problems their presence may create will usually be minor ones. In addition to the briefings on the larger affairs of state and the UN debates, they will want to know where to eat in New York for the same price they enjoy in the parliamentary dining room, or how their home-town newspaper (from Moose Jaw or Antigonish) can be found in New York on the day of publication, or how to get a ticket for that night's performance of a long-sold-out play. There's a lost wallet here, a parking ticket there, a piece of luggage gone astray — and sometimes MPs lose their way, but, by the time the General Assembly finally ends, we are sorry to see them go.

Only rarely do our parliamentary kinfolk become involved in some untoward incident — of such a nature as to go unrecorded in the omnivorous files of External Affairs —

such as what happened to a certain MP, who shall remain unnamed. This man came to New York as an observer on the Canadian Delegation to the United Nations General Assembly in an autumn of the early 1970s.

Short in stature, dark of hair, high of spirit and quick of tongue, he brought to New York his spouse, a lady considerably taller than he and, by contrast, blonde. To forestall any suggestion here of male chauvinism, let an understatement suffice that she was a stunner, a showstopper — altogether glorious to behold.

To parliamentarians and others from Ottawa coming down to help out at the General Assembly, Canada's Permanent Mission used to put them up at the Barclay Hotel — a dignified hostelry located next to the Waldorf Astoria in the block between Park and Lexington Avenues and between 48th and 49th Streets. During that autumn, a store across the road from the Lexington Avenue entrance to the Barclay had closed, leaving a dark stretch on this busy and otherwise brightly lit thoroughfare. That dark stretch began to attract a considerable number of Ladies of the Night, seeking to maintain a low profile and to avoid harassment by New York's Finest, who were on one of their periodic rampages to reduce such blemishes on the Big Apple's image.

However, to the growing consternation of the Barclay's management, not only did these ladies continue to congregate on Lexington Avenue right across the road from the hotel entrance, but, it was noticed, on occasion a Barclay guest would conduct one upstairs in the hotel.

To thwart this unprecedented threat to the Barclay's reputation, the management set up security desks inside the hotel's entrances and manned these with house detectives whose roster was augmented so that a watch could be kept up around the clock.

It was during this period that our parliamentary observer followed the proceedings of a UN committee well into the evening hours. Very tired, he was then joined by his wife for a late snack, and they strolled together back to the

Barclay. Mounting the steps leading to the lobby, our MP was accosted by a recently hired house detective who took him aside.

The following dialogue ensued.

Friendly House Detective, in a very discreet voice:
  "Sorry, sir, may I ask you not to take this woman upstairs."
Parliamentarian, somewhat less discreetly:
  "And just why, may I ask, should I not take this woman upstairs?"
Friendly House Detective, still discreetly:
  "Please understand, sir, I'm just doing my job. And that's to ask you to not take this woman upstairs."
Parliamentarian, not at all discreetly:
  "I'll have you know that this woman is my wife, living with me in the hotel, and I'm damned well going to take her upstairs."
Friendly House Detective, looking from short parliamentarian to Statuesque Companion with a tut-tut, where-have-I-heard-this-one-before air:
  "Sure, I understand sir, but I must still ask you not to take her upstairs."
Statuesque Companion, seemingly amused, remains aloof from conversation.
Parliamentarian, colour approaching purple:
  "I'm a member of the Canadian Delegation to the United Nations. Here's my Delegation identification card. And any member of the Delegation staying at the hotel will certainly identify my wife."
Friendly House Detective, beginning to frown, casts quick look around lobby. Not a member of the Delegation is in sight.
Parliamentarian, irate:
  "Phone anyone at the Canadian Permanent Mission. They will confirm that this is my wife." He pulls out a copy of the Permanent Mission's home telephone list (with which we thoughtfully arm all parliamentary visitors).

Friendly House Detective, by now alarmed, phones Angus
   Matheson, head of chancery.

Angus, as stolid and phlegmatic a Scot as ever worked for
External, was fortunately at home. Asked by the house
detective to describe the parliamentarian's wife, Angus — a
specialist in External's and the United Nations' budget and
finances — rose to the challenge. His description, with his
customary regard for detail, of the parliamentarian's handsome wife satisfied the house detective completely.

Statuesque Companion, to parliamentarian: "Well, thank
   God that's over. Now let's get upstairs and go to bed."

A Mix-Up
in the Mail

Whenever I get mad at the post office — when I learn, for instance, that a letter has taken ten days to reach Toronto from Ottawa, first-class — I think back to even more bizarre events enveloping my wife's mail in New York City in 1944. I was at the Canadian Consulate General in New York at the time.

The Second World War was approaching its climax, and Crenia was working for the American Industries War Salvage Committee, an outfit created by the National Association of Manufacturers to promote the saving of scrap metal by householders nation-wide.

Crenia ran this salvage campaign from a one-room office on a lower floor of the 102-storey Empire State Building, then the highest office tower in the world, and one of the grandest. Unbeknownst to her, on a floor high above were the imposing offices of Celanese Corp., a far-flung conglomerate enterprise, headed in the United States by Sir Samuel Salvage. Its headquarters were in London.

Crenia started her scrap-collecting campaign by setting up voluntary committees in communities across the nation. To inspire them to ever new heights, she created a little weekly

28

paper called *The Scrapper*. She sent it to local communities
and to newspapers far and wide.

Our best friend in New York at the time was a cartoonist,
Elliot Caplin, who happened to be a young brother of the
creator (Al Capp) of the famous comic strip Li'l Abner. Overshadowed by his brother, Elliot Caplin started his career by
pioneering in adapting cartoons and comic strips for educational purposes, in popular magazines and for the armed
forces.

On Crenia's request, Elliot came up with the idea of
creating Salvage Sam. In comic strip form every week in *The
Scrapper*, Salvage Sam would show Americans in the
boondocks how they could help win the war by turning in
old cans, empty tins and bottle tops to their local scrap
committees.

Not long after Salvage Sam was launched, a strange thing
began happening in the mail. In their nether regions of the

Empire State Building, Crenia and Elliot — Salvage Sam's parents — were puzzled to receive letters in *The Scrapper* office inviting "Sir Samuel" to tea at the Harvard Club, or to dinner with Oxford and Cambridge graduates in the metropolitan area. One day an embossed invitation arrived, inviting Sir Samuel to the annual dinner of the Pilgrim's Society. It impressed the occupants of *The Scrapper's* office no end.

Meanwhile, in the Celanese Corp. offices in the posh penthouse floors of the Empire State, Sir Samuel Salvage began receiving no less puzzling mail. It would say things like "Great tip you gave us on garbage can tops last week, Sam," and "Good idea, Sam. You've helped push Walla Walla to meet its goal on bottle tops," and "S.S., should we step on tin cans to straighten them out before turning them in?"

It took some undercover investigation and a diplomatic intermediary (me) to get this little mail mess straightened out. Regretfully, Salvage Sam on the second floor and Sir Samuel Salvage on the ninety-second never did meet one another formally. I don't know what became of Celanese's Sir Samuel, but Salvage Sam's creator went on to outdo his famous brother and today, under pseudonyms, is the creator of half a dozen leading comic strips. As for Crenia, she was soon plunged into even more bizarre hazards of spousedom in *la vie diplomatique*.

Ireland

A Case of
Mistaken Identity

None of the homework that my wife, Crenia, and I did in anticipation of our three-year posting to Ireland prepared us, in any way, for what was to happen one night in 1959, at a black-tie dinner at the official residence of the French ambassador in Dublin.

In the late autumn of that year Jack Lynch was appointed minister of industry and commerce in the Irish cabinet — he was later to become prime minister of Ireland — and I began to realize that we had a strong facial resemblance. Furthermore, we were approximately the same build, with similarly receding hairlines, and we were both inveterate pipe smokers. I was serving as counsellor — Number Two — at the Canadian Embassy in Dublin at the time.

Mr Lynch had been attracting more and more public attention and seemed destined to be a rising star in the governing Fianna Fail Party. As for me, I noticed that at Dublin Castle and at public functions elsewhere in the Irish capital, news photographers occasionally mistook me for the popular cabinet minister. For example, one night at a gala performance of the visiting Royal Ballet, I was once more startled when, descending a staircase at intermission, pho-

tographers called out to me with,"Hold it a minute, Mr
Lynch." It was becoming a habit.

One day when my ambassador was absent from Ireland
and I was serving as chargé d'affaires of the embassy, a
formidable and impeccably crafted card from the French
ambassador was delivered to our home. It invited the chargé
d'affaires of Canada and Mrs Freifeld to a black-tie dinner the
following week "in honour of the newly appointed Irish
minister of industry and commerce and Mrs Jack Lynch."

The French ambassador, M. le Comte de Blesson, was a
member of his country's aristocracy, and he was a tall, austere, forbidding diplomat. By virtue of his length of service
as ambassador in Dublin, he was also dean of the diplomatic
corps. He was noted for the fastidiousness and meticulous-
ness of his entertaining no less than for the culinary accomplishments of his French chef. An invitation to dine at the
French Embassy residence was cherished by Dubliners and,
indeed, by members of our local diplomatic community.

Like good punctual Canadians, and mindful that I was not
yet of ambassadorial rank as the other guests would doubtless be, Crenia and I arrived at the French Embassy residence
promptly — only a few moments after the designated hour
of 7 p.m. From the diplomatic plates on the cars outside, we
could see that two or three couples had already arrived and,
when the butler opened the door for us, we could see M. de
Blesson busy chatting with them.

To our surprise, however, on seeing us in the doorway, the
ambassador dropped his guests like hotcakes, came to the
door to greet us effusively, escort us inside and present us to
the others as his guests of honour for the evening — the
newly appointed Irish minister of industry and commerce
and Mrs Jack Lynch!

The other guests knew who we were, or certainly knew
that we were *not* Mr and Mrs Lynch. But they, like ourselves,
must have been too surprised and embarrassed to react
other than passively. Assuming it to be simply a momen-
tary lapse, none of us ventured to correct our forbidding

host. Nor was the ambassadress around to whisper in his ear and put him straight; notwithstanding her chef's punc- tilliousness, she was in the habit of lingering in the kitchen to supervise until shortly before the guests were to go in to dinner.

When more guests arrived at the door, the ambassador left it to his butler to bring them in while he continued to hover around us. And, to our growing consternation, when he got around to presenting the newcomers to us, he continued to call us his guests of honour, the minister of industry and commerce and Mrs Lynch.

The front doorbell rang once more and — to our intense relief — in came the real Irish minister of industry and commerce and the real Mrs Lynch. Their appearance at long last would surely, we thought, end the confusion. But, to our astonishment and dismay, the ambassador presented *them* to *us* as the chargé d'affaires of Canada and Mrs Freifeld! Again, it must have been the element of surprise and embar- rassment that deterred the Lynches as well as ourselves, from seeking to correct our host. More cocktails and canapés circulated.

We found it difficult to believe that our host's aberration could continue any longer — but it did. It then began to dawn on my wife — looking at the clock and in near shock at the thought that dinner must be only a few moments away — that the ambassador would be escorting her into the dining room and seating her on his right and that the ambas- sadress would expect to find me on her right — place cards and *plan de table* notwithstanding. The Lynches, if this nonsense continued, would doubtless find themselves being seated at some remote part of the twenty-four-place table, befitting a mere Canadian chargé.

Appalled at such a prospect and feeling an unease border- ing on panic, Crenia decided that something drastic had to be done — and done fast.

Looking around the salon, which by now was filled with guests with cocktails in hand, she noticed our host huddled in quiet conversation with the senior Irish diplomatic official present, Jack Molloy. At that time he was assistant under-secretary at the Irish foreign office and soon to be appointed ambassador to the Court of St. James.

Our wives don't require specific protocol instructions or long diplomatic exposure to know that, at such a gathering, when your host is off in a corner engaged in an ostensibly private business conversation with a high foreign ministry official, it would be the path of wisdom not to interrupt. And Crenia, herself a rather reserved and unaggressive person, would be about the least likely diplomatic wife to do so. But with D-hour imminent, she decided that barge in she must.

Working her way over to their quiet corner, she inserted herself athwart the ambassador and Mr Molloy and, at the first pause in their conversation and in a complete non-sequitur, broke in with:"You know, at home in Canada, we must be having snow already at this time of year."

At this interruption, Ambassador de Blesson turned to her, with an odd look coming over his eyes. She plunged bravely on: "In my country, in our part of *Canada*, winter starts early. Back home in *Ottawa*, there must be snow on the ground already."

The odd look in the ambassador's eyes turned into a frown, then into a deep scowl, and he didn't say a word. Without explanation, he detached himself from Jack Molloy and Crenia and, when dinner was announced a few moments later, with all graciousness and as though noth-ing had happened, he took Mrs Lynch's arm and escorted her to her place at the table, the chair on his right. By this time Mme de Blesson had emerged from her kitchen and, quite unaware of what had been going on, went down to her end of the table escorted by the newly appointed Irish minister of industry and commerce, who was duly seated on her right.

As for the Canadian chargé d'affaires and *his* wife, they were seated, as planned, in the bleachers — diplomatically speaking— and they were never invited back to the French

Embassy, not even for the customary large reception on *Quatorze Juillet*.

To this day I don't know whether my double, who soon became Taoiseach — prime minister — of Ireland, ever found out what or who was causing the confusion at that black-tie dinner in his honour at the Official Residence of the Ambassador Plenipotentiary and Extraordinary of France and *Doyen du Corps Diplomatique* in convivial Dublin back in 1959.

Diefenbaker's "Champagne"

On a January morning in 1961 a cipher telegram from External Affairs in Ottawa arrived at the Canadian Embassy in Dublin. It informed us that, in response to an earlier invitation, Prime Minister John Diefenbaker, accompanied by Mrs Diefenbaker, would make an official trip to Ireland on Sunday and Monday, March 5 and 6, if those days were convenient to the Irish prime minister. They were.

External's telegram informed us also that the Diefenbakers would arrive in Dublin following a short visit to Belfast, and that they would then be going on to London where Mr Diefenbaker would attend a Commonwealth Prime Ministers' Conference.

As soon as this message was deciphered, I — as chargé d'affaires — decided to telephone our ambassador, Alfred Rive, who was vacationing on the Continent, to give him this important news. At the same time, I urged him to complete his vacation so that we could utilize the intervening time to get on with the preliminary preparations.

From the moment the ambassador returned, he emphasized that Mr Diefenbaker was a teetotaller and that we must direct our planning to minimize, if we could not eliminate

38

entirely, any exposure of our prime minister to alcohol — no small feat in convivial Ireland.

Although the Diefenbakers were originally scheduled to arrive on a Canadian government plane at 11 a.m. on a Sunday, Mr Rive contrived an opportunity to delay the arrival until 2:15 p.m. His ploy was to ensure that our teetotalling prime minister's first function, after the arrival ceremonies at the airport, would be *tea* at the embassy residence, to which Dublin's Canadian colony and our embassy staff would be invited. This manoeuvre, as it turned out, was successful.

Mr Diefenbaker agreed that he and the Canadian official party would be housed, like other visiting heads of government, at the Shelbourne Hotel, a fine old Dublin hostelry on St. Stephen's Green, just across the square from Iveagh House, headquarters of the Irish Ministry of External Affairs. Thus it would be at the Shelbourne Hotel that Mr Diefenbaker would give the official Canadian reception.

The moment this was decided, Mr Rive began scouring the Shelbourne Hotel for a suitable room for this affair. To our surprise, he turned down those that seemed obviously right and that were constantly used for this purpose. We finally realized that he was seeking a large room in the shape of an L; his gambit was that Mr Diefenbaker would receive his guests at the top of the L while the bar — which the ambassador unhappily agreed could not be eliminated — would be around the corner at the other end of the L and, at least, out of sight and smell of our prime minister.

And so the planning went — with the ambassador preoccupied continuously about how to minimize his teetotalling Chief's exposure within Ireland to whiskey, wine and Guinness Stout.

Then, a couple of days before the visit was due to commence, still another telegram came in from Ottawa, signed "Robinson." It was from Basil Robinson, the top-echelon External Affairs officer, who at that time was serving as the Department's special assistant in the prime minister's office. When this was deciphered I could hardly believe what I read: "BEST WAY TO ENSURE SUCCESSFUL VISIT IS TO MAKE CERTAIN THAT CHAMPAGNE GETS FROM AIR-PORT TO SHELBOURNE AHEAD OF PRIME MINISTER."

I rushed to the ambassador's office and exclaimed: "Have you seen this incredible telegram from Basil? Here we have been going crazy for a month trying to keep the prime minister removed from alcohol, and they are bringing their own champagne on the official plane! Apart from the PM's teetotallism, one just doesn't do such a thing. Can't they trust us to procure in Dublin any drink they might require?"

The perplexed ambassador, sensitive that it had been he who had been fussing for weeks about how to keep alcohol away from Mr Diefenbaker, put in a transatlantic telephone call to Basil Robinson. When he had finished the call, he came out to us grinning and, ever so gently, told us that Basil had explained that CHAMPAGNE (our telegrams at that time were reproduced entirely in upper case) was not a beverage but the name of the confidential messenger, Gilbert Cham-pagne. This "messenger" had been serving Canadian prime ministers ever since the days of Sir Robert Borden. For the first time, he was being taken on a trip abroad by Mr Diefen-baker. It was important to get Champagne — the man — to the Shelbourne Hotel with the prime minister's luggage, while the arrival ceremonies were going on at the airport, so that he could have fresh clothes laid out for Mr Diefenbaker for the quick change that he would have to make before going on to his first function.

Afterwards, I learned that similar confusion had arisen the previous day in Belfast. In his autobiography, Mr Diefen-baker recounts that a telegram from his office to Belfast: PRIME MINISTER WILL BE BRINGING CHAMPAGNE, appeared to annoy the Canadian officials in Northern Ireland who were preparing for his visit. They apparently feared that Dief was questioning the quality of champagne in Ulster and that he was initiating the practice, internationally, of B.Y.O.L. Mr Diefenbaker writes that, in Belfast, they even had a panel truck, equipped with wine racks, wheeled out on the tarmac "to accommodate our Champagne" as soon as his plane landed. In Dublin, we, by then forewarned, had a stationwagon ready at the airport to rush (Mr) Champagne to the Shelbourne Hotel.

Although they may not have realized it at the time, Mr Diefenbaker and Basil Robinson had provided us with a welcome diversion from the weighty briefs we had been preparing for Canada's prime minister on Irish nationalism, partition, President De Valera and the Gaelic Revival.

For Want of
a (Wing) Collar

Working in the Canadian foreign service may be occasionally enlivened by some crisis over clothing — more frequently over the clothing of your visiting minister or prime minister than over your own. Clothing crises can overtake anyone, but somehow they take on a more comical aspect if, for example, the locale is Buckingham Palace and the occasion is an Annual Reception given by Their Majesties for the diplomatic corps. Here, in 1957, the wife of an aide to High Commissioner George Drew, finding that her long dress was being trampled as the line of diplomats moved forward to be presented, gathered up what she thought was her hem, only to find that she held in her hand the tails of the glowering Libyan ambassador.

Or, in 1954, if the locale is Lutyens Palace, former residence of British Viceroys in New Delhi, and the occasion is the White Tie and Decorations dinner about to be offered by Prime Minister Nehru in honour of Canadian Prime Minister Louis St. Laurent, who was making an around-the-world official tour. One of our assistant under-secretaries, Charles Ritchie, who was accompanying Mr St. Laurent, was called to the prime minister's bedroom and found him standing in full white-tie regalia, but no trousers; they had been left on the plane. As Ritchie relates in his wonderful diaries: "Every-one else had his trousers, but the Prime Minister was trouser-less. Like Sir Walter Raleigh throwing down his cloak for Queen Elizabeth to walk upon, I said 'Take mine, Prime Minister,' but a second look at his girth and mine showed that this was a physical impossibility." The crisis was resolved, in a manner of speaking, by sending a servant to the nearest bazaar. He returned with "an extremely greasy pair of sec-ond- or third-hand trousers of such circumference that they had to be fastened around the Prime Minister's waist with safety pins."

When I was serving at our embassy in Dublin, we had a little prime-ministerial clothing crisis of our own — involving nothing so crucial as Liberal trousers, but a Conservative wing collar. This was during Mr Diefenbaker's official visit to the Irish capital when our ambassador, Alfred Rive, con-trived to have the first function attended by our teetotalling PM — a tea for the Canadian community at the embassy residence — out in the Dublin suburbs. This affair was proceeding swimmingly, when Mr Rive received an urgent telephone call from the PM's special assistant, Basil Robin-son, who had remained in town at the Hotel Shelbourne to work on telegrams. Also at the hotel, the prime minister's confidential messenger, Gilbert Champagne, was laying out Mr Diefenbaker's clothing for the White Tie and Decorations dinner that Irish Prime Minister Sean Lemass would be giv-ing in his honour in a couple of hours.

To Basil's and Champagne's horror — no wing collars; they had been left behind in Belfast, and finding a haber-dashery open in Dublin on a Sunday afternoon in 1961 was as improbable as finding one open in Toronto on a Sunday in the '30s.

On the telephone, Basil asked Mr Rive whether his collar size was the same as Mr Diefenbaker's. It was not, and nor was mine. At that moment Forman, the somewhat ancient waiter used at many functions in Dublin's small diplomatic community, hovered into view bearing a tray loaded with tea and sandwiches — and a slightly soiled wing collar around his neck! Mr Rive, to Forman's astonishment, asked his collar size. Glory be — the same as Mr Diefenbaker's. Mr Rive asked Forman for the urgent loan of his collar and said he could stop serving immediately and go home. When Mr Rive explained, in a whisper, the nature of the emergency, Forman coolly took a collar out of his pocket and handed it to the ambassador. "I always carry a spare. My compliments to the Prime Minister of Canada."

At the gala dinner that evening Crenia and I noted that Forman's wing collar reposed comfortably on the prime ministerial neck — and Mr Diefenbaker was none the wiser.

Less critical, perhaps, was what befell our commercial counsellor in Bogota, Jim Elliot, who was serving as chargé d'affaires while I (by then, ambassador) was absent from the country. In the middle of the morning, he suddenly received a call from Colombian Protocol saying the diplomatic corps was being invited to attend a requiem mass at the Cathedral that noon. Jim used to rent formal clothing, and for this occasion he sent our driver to pick up morning coat and striped trousers. (His size was kept in the renting store's file along with the size of all other regular diplomatic clients.) Making a last-minute change of clothes at the office before being driven to the cathedral, Jim, a burly fellow, was shaken to discover that the sleeves of his morning coat came down barely to his elbows.

But there was no time to go to the store and change. Descending from his car at the cathedral, Jim saw the miniscule Chinese ambassador getting out of his car, with the sleeves of *his* jacket nearly reaching the ground. They laughed at what must have happened back in the store, quickly changed morning coats and, impeccably garbed, strode with appropriately sombre mien to their seats for the requiem mass.

Russia
and China

Soviet Intelligence?

Although newspapers at the time did not report it, and no mention of it is to be found in External Affairs' files, the USSR's vaunted intelligence apparatus seemed, curiously, to have failed for a few days back in 1971. This is what happened.

Mr Trudeau was making the first official visit to the Soviet Union by a Canadian prime minister and, for the occasion, was accompanied by a small bevy of aides. Foremost among them was an old External colleague, Marshall Crowe, who by 1971 had risen to an exalted position in the Canadian public service — deputy secretary of the Canadian cabinet and assistant clerk of the privy council. If for no other reason, he was a figure on whom the Soviet Union's bureaucracy would assuredly be expected to maintain a curriculum vitae in their omnivorous files.

But there were more important reasons. Marshall had worked in earlier years in the Department of External Affairs and had served as USSR desk officer in External's Eastern European Division. That job had brought him into frequent contact with the Soviet Union's big embassy in Ottawa, which would certainly have compiled a detailed profile on him for the foreign ministry — and the KGB — in Moscow.

Furthermore, he had served a full tour of duty at the Canadian Embassy in Moscow; any minor blank about him in Soviet files would certainly have been filled in while he was there.

You do not have to be an intelligence specialist or one of John le Carré's characters to be certain that the Soviet authorities, long before Marshall's visit to Moscow with Mr Trudeau, would have had data on every facet of Marshall Crowe's background — his character, foibles, education and Canadian public service career.

Furthermore, when an official visit of a high personage is impending, profile sketches of the visitors and the key people they will be meeting are updated and exchanged between the two countries. Thus, when Mr Trudeau and his party arrived in Moscow, Marshall had no reason to believe that his hosts would not know precisely who he was.

The first night in Moscow Mr Trudeau and his party were the guests of honour at an official dinner offered by Prime Minister Alexei Kosygin and attended by a panoply of the Soviet Union's top political personages and military brass. For this occasion Marshall, and the other Canadians, wore ordinary, dark, business suits; white ties and decorations, or even black tie, are not worn at such state functions in the USSR.

When he was seated, Marshall was surprised to find that he was not located together with his USSR opposite number or comparable Soviet official. And he became positively astonished to see, as the guests took their seats, that he was being flanked by a full marshal of the Soviet Union, the USSR's highest military rank, and a Soviet colonel-general, a rank higher than any in the Canadian Armed Forces. Our Marshall noted with surprise that these gentlemen were not clothed in business suits but were in beribboned uniforms, bedecked with medals, befitting heroes of their exalted rank.

If this clutch of Soviet High Brass were puzzled at finding Canada's plainclothed and unbemedalled Marshall seated in their midst, they were too polite to show it. When they realized from preliminary small-talk that Marshall spoke their native tongue, they seemed pleased, and the one-L marshal of the Soviet Union soon asked Canada's two-L Marshall what was the largest number of divisions of the valiant Canadian Army that he had had under his command during World War II. Marshall replied: "By the end of the war, I had risen to the rank of captain and the largest number of men I ever commanded during the war was a platoon of nineteen."

From the looks on the faces of the Russian officers, it seemed they had begun to realize that Canada's Marshall, somehow, was not like theirs. And perhaps because they had begun also to realize what a blooper had been made by their side — by those *nudniks* of the Party bureaucracy and the KGB — they seemed amused. They began to display as much *bonhomie* to our mere captain as they might have shown to an officer of their own lofty rank.

In the growing conviviality, Marshall Crowe soon thought it appropriate to put a question to the marshal of the Soviet Union. What was the *smallest* number of men the distinguished marshal had commanded during World War II?

Out came the crisp reply: "An Army!" Everyone joined in the laughter.

This strange state of affairs persisted when Mr Trudeau and his party visited Kiev. At the official dinner in that city in honour of the Canadian prime minister, Marshall Crowe — in his dark business suit — again found himself flanked by redoubtable, beribboned, bemedalled, Soviet Highest Brass. Incredibly, the word had *not* been passed along from Moscow to Kiev.

Which led Marshall and I to speculate, when he told me this story, whether the USSR bureaucracy, with its sinuous intelligence apparatus, are as omniscient as we in the West have so long been prone to believe.

The Howling Cats
of Moscow

External Affairs wives and husbands come
from all walks of Canadian life and their performance abroad
reflects their varied background. Some — and these are
likely to be of an older generation — are happy to share with
their spouses the burdens of official entertainment, showing
the flag, assisting the local Canadian colony's charitable and
social endeavours, and winning friends and influencing people for Canada. Others might shun such duties in favour of
pursuing their own interests or career to the extent that is
possible in the country where they are stationed. There is
one complaint that all share in common — the lack of
recognition by headquarters for jobs well done and services
rendered for Canada.

And sometimes a foreign service spouse succeeds in
accomplishing something with the local authorities in which
the Externalite and the embassy staff have gotten nowhere.
Take, for example, the case of the redoubtable Teresa Ford,
whose husband was Canada's outstanding ambassador to
the Soviet Union during sixteen rugged years.

Teresa was not one to suffer the vicissitudes of life in the
Communist paradise with reticence — especially in the matter of the nocturnal howling of Moscow's hordes of stray

cats which, colleagues who have served there assert, was particularly obnoxious in the vicinity of the Canadian Embassy.

For years the Canadian Embassy had urged Moscow's local authorities and the USSR Ministry of Foreign Affairs to do something — anything — to alleviate this plague. The Canadian entreaties and complaints had accomplished precisely nothing. If anything, as the months rolled by, the cats were multiplying at an alarming rate and their howling was becoming more dreadful than ever.

Teresa was worried not so much about the disturbance to her own sleep as the effect it would have on her hard-working husband. At three o'clock one morning Teresa was wakened by feline howling of unprecedented intensity and, in exasperation, she determined to try a new approach with the Russians, the hour notwithstanding.

She dialed the telephone number of George Costakis, a locally engaged clerk at the embassy (who was subsequently to achieve world renown in art circles for the magnificent collection of early Russian avant-garde paintings that he had quietly acquired through the years).

When George sleepily answered the phone, Teresa said to him: "George, I want you to call protocol immediately, *immediately*. And I want you to tell protocol that if the Soviet Union can put astronaut Yuri Gargarin into outer space, it can surely do something about these damned cats that are driving us crazy at the embassy."

George Costakis wearily hung up the phone with the promise to make still another plea to the authorities. He did not call protocol at three o'clock in the morning, but he did call as soon as the USSR Ministry of Foreign Affairs opened. He told the most senior functionary he could get on the phone: "The Ambassadress of Canada has instructed me to tell you that if the Soviet Union can succeed in putting Yuri Gargarin into orbit, can it not do something about the cats around the Canadian Embassy that are driving us all crazy?"

Whether it was because the Russian *amour propre* was

piqued or whether the Ministry was astonished at this novel Canadian approach, it did do something. That same day a small army of *dvorniks* showed up around the Canadian Embassy with brooms and long staves and soon cleared the area of its feline bestiary. That night — for the first time in weeks — the Fords and their staff enjoyed an uninterrupted night's slumber.

For the VIP
who has
Everything

When a prime minister makes an official visit overseas, the planners in Ottawa find that not the least of the diplomatic problems is deciding what gifts Canada's PM should bestow on foreign hosts.

The planners will almost certainly reject what Prime Minister John Diefenbaker used to do — present an autographed glossy print of himself to his hosts in far-off lands. Surely we can do a little better than that, they will say: something not too extravagant, distinctively Canadian and unlikely ever to have been given before. But if the visit is something special — as Prime Minister Pierre Trudeau's was when he went to Peking (Beijing) in 1973 — how will they equal the present from the people of Canada to the leaders of a billion Chinese?

Back in 1973, Mr Trudeau's planners in External Affairs were undoubtedly aware that, for years, Canadian zoos had been trying to induce the Chinese to give them a pair of pandas, a species nearing extinction, or the almost-as-rare Manchurian snow leopard. Perhaps it was the subconscious wish that our Chinese hosts would donate one of these rare beasts to Canada that inspired External Affairs to come up with a truly ingenious idea — Mr Trudeau should present a live animal in Peking.

Now what animal is eminently Canadian? inexpensive and easy to obtain? and has never before been presented to a foreign government by a Canadian prime minister? You guessed it: the beaver, and not one, but four — two males and two females.

This innovative proposal received quick prime-ministerial blessing and an enthusiastic endorsement from a surprised John Small, Canada's ambassador in Peking. So the planners next attacked the problems of procurement and logistics, including how to keep the sluggish beasts alive and happy during the long journey.

Advice and assistance was sought from fellow bureaucrats in the Department of Indian and Northern Affairs (INA). Finally, when all the loose ends of beaver-giving were tied together, External sent a telegram to the Canadian Embassy in Peking, with a copy for the embassy in Tokyo, where the Trudeau party would stop en route.

To preserve the element of surprise in the Chinese capital, they sent this telegram in cipher:

FROM EXTERNAL OTTAWA SEPT. 28/73
TO PEKING
REF: PM'S VISIT — ANIMAL PRESENTATIONS.

1. FOUR BEAVERS ARRIVING ON PM'S AIRCRAFT WILL NEED TO BE FED. INA REPORTS FOLLOWING KINDS OF FOOD SUITABLE: (A) POPULUS (POPLAR), (B) SALIX (WILLOWS), (C) RUBIS (RASPBERRIES), (D) NUPHAR (WATERLILIES), (E) BETULA (BIRCH); UNDERSTAND HYACINTH AVAILABLE IN CHINA COULD PROBABLY REPLACE WATERLILIES IF, AFTER TASTING, BEAVERS LIKE CHINESE FOOD. WE WILL SEND 50-POUND BAG OF ALFALFA TO SUSTAIN THEM UNTIL LOCAL FOOD SUPPLY OBTAINED.
2. AS BEAVERS ONLY DEFECATE IN WATER AND HOLD BACK DURING JOURNEY THEY SHOULD BE PLACED IN POOL OF WATER ON ARRIVAL TO PROVIDE RELIEF AND PREVENT POSSIBLE CRITICAL CONDITION, ESPECIALLY AFTER SUCH LONG FLIGHT.

3. GRATEFUL YOU DESIGNATE MEMBER EMBASSY STAFF AS BEAVER
LIAISON OFFICER.
4. FOR TOKYO: BEAVERS WILL REMAIN ON AIRCRAFT DURING
STOPOVER. GRATEFUL YOU ADVISE JAPANESE AUTHORITIES.

The person to whom Ambassador Small entrusted the delicate chore of Embassy Beaver Liaison Officer was its resident sinologist, Brian Evans, a professor of history from the University of Alberta. Having made this choice, the embassy then sent this telegram to External Affairs in Ottawa:

FROM PEKING OCT. 5/73
TO EXTERNAL OTTAWA.
REF: YOUR TEL SEPT. 28
PM'S VISIT — ANIMAL PRESENTATIONS.

BEAVER LIAISON OFFICER WOULD LIKE THE FOLLOWING INFO:
(A) WHAT ARE MINIMUM REQUIREMENTS FOR BEAVER ZOO
PENS?
(B) WHAT ARE OPTIMUM REQUIREMENTS FOR BEAVER ZOO
PENS?
(C) IF POSSIBLE, CAN YOU SEND WITH BEAVERS THE
FOLLOWING:
RELEVANT LITERATURE SUCH AS: TEACH YOURSELF BEAVERS;
EVERYTHING YOU EVER WANTED TO KNOW ABOUT BEAVERS
BUT WERE AFRAID TO ASK.
(D) ANY SHORT FILM ON BEAVERS.
(E) TAPE OF PETER GZOWSKI'S CBC SHOW DEVOTED TO
BEAVERS.

The beavers survived the journey and were presented by Mr Trudeau to Chou En-Lai, who accepted them on behalf of the government and people of China.

The beavers, or their offspring, are living it up in the Peking Zoo today and have doubtless acquired a taste for Chinese food such as hyacinth.

Canadian zoos, however, are still awaiting a pair of pandas or Manchurian snow leopards from the friends the prime minister is supposed to have made in China.

Ottawa and Headquarters

Our Illegal
Declaration of War

Canadians, and perhaps the rest of the world, may be surprised to learn that, strictly speaking, Canada entered World War II in an illegal and unconstitutional manner.

The blame, in retrospect, must be placed on some very wise and dedicated men who, in the late summer of 1939, were being worked to, and beyond, their limit in the Department of External Affairs. And they were harassed by an astute but impatient prime minister, Mackenzie King, who, to make matters more difficult, served also as his own secretary of state for external affairs.

His principal adviser and under-secretary of state for external affairs was O.D. Skelton, under whom served a galaxy of distinguished Canadians including John Read, who was legal adviser, Norman Robertson, Hugh Keenleyside, Loring Christie and, over at Canada House in London, Vincent Massey and Lester B. ("Mike") Pearson. This is what happened:

On September 1, 1939, as the Externalites had feared, Hitler's war machine attacked Poland. On September 3, Britain declared war on Germany and was joined promptly by New Zealand and Australia. Meanwhile Prime Minister

King had summoned parliament — which had been in summer recess — to discuss the question of Canada entering the
war and parliament's verdict, about which there had been
little doubt, was to proclaim entry into the war forthwith.

As planned in External Affairs, this triggered a mid-day
September 9 cable to London — where it was already evening — instructing Canadian High Commissioner Vincent
Massey to inform the King that an important document
would be submitted shortly for His Majesty's immediate
approval. This was soon followed by a cable conveying the
text of the war proclamation.

When it arrived in London, it was late night. Canada
House's sole, haggard cipher clerk, who hadn't seen his
family for a week and whose wife was to be evacuated to the
country the next day, arranged to be awakened at seven the
next morning, September 10, to unscramble the crucial text.

Back in Ottawa, Skelton and most of External had stayed
up through the night, badgered constantly by an impatient
Mackenzie King, awaiting word about His Majesty's signature on the war proclamation.

When the cable was unscrambled early on September 10
in London, Mike Pearson was informed of its contents and
quickly sought an audience for High Commissioner Massey
with the King. But the King's private secretary couldn't be
located at the moment, and Pearson was then told that the
proclamation would be signed after the King had returned
from a day out at Windsor Castle.

At this point Massey intervened. He insisted on an
audience with the King forthwith at Windsor Castle. He
hastily scrawled the deciphered text of Canada's war proclamation on a couple of sheets of paper and rushed out to
Windsor in his son's sports car. The King signed Massey's
handwritten text, External was informed by cable and the
government ordered publication in the *Canada Gazette* of
the declaration of war.

There were only two things the matter with External's
well-laid plan. The King had approved a proclamation lack-

ing the signature of his Canadian prime minister. And the Canadian prime minister had ordered publication in the *Canada Gazette* of a proclamation lacking the signature of the King.

This had not the slightest effect on Canada's subsequent prosecution of the war, and the not-unimportant formalities were properly completed in subsequent weeks — leaving jurists and diplomats to ponder when, in fact, Canada legally entered the war.

And if specialists in historic documents are now pondering — on reading this tale from External Affairs — what Vincent Massey's little pieces of paper, with King George VI's signature, might fetch today at auction in Christie's or Sotheby's, they should save themselves the trouble. Prime Minister King, with an avid interest in historic objects, instructed External to secure from Massey those pieces of paper with the scribbled war proclamation signed on September 10, 1939, by the King; they belonged, the PM asserted, in Canada's archives.

Not so, asserted Vincent Massey (who was no less aware of the value of historic documents than his boss); the sheets had no constitutional standing and certainly should not be placed in any official file. At one point in this curious impasse, External's legal adviser, John Read, went so far as to counsel the prime minister that, to gain possession of those sheets, he should either recall Massey and charge him under the Defence Regulations or get him some sort of honorific title.

King and Canada's Public Archives never did secure those pieces of paper on the basis of which — some persons may still maintain — Canada "illegally" entered the Second World War. To this day they have not been recovered.

The Penny-Pincher
of External

The guided-tour visitors that crowd External Affairs' opulent and overcrowded new building on Ottawa's Sussex Drive would not find credible the unbelievable penury in which the Department had to operate in its earlier years. In fact, even its unkindest critics might be surprised to learn that, until the '60s, External was crimpingly preoccupied with how to save the taxpayer's dollar all the time it was devising Canada's foreign policy.

The Czar — rather Czarina — of External's early finances and administration was not a scion of the Romanov dynasty or a Rockcliffe mandarin but a schoolteacher from Chesterville, Ontario, by the name of Kathryn Agnes McCloskey. Although first hired as a "lady typewriter" shortly after the Department was created in 1909, she soon became the autocrat of its puny finances — refusing to dispense so much as a new pencil to a secretary unless she got back a stub she considered short enough to replace. Both sides and the margins of every page of our stenographers' notebooks would meet Agnes's scrutiny to ensure that the hapless creatures had exhausted every square inch before she would provide a new one.

Although, when she rose to "Principal Clerk," Agnes did

not rank high in External's early pecking order, she managed to occupy choice space — the under-secretary's fine, outer office on the second floor of Parliament Hill's East Block. Norman Robertson, probably our greatest under-secretary and Prime Minister King's trusted adviser, found Agnes's interference with his flow of paper so obtrusive that he attempted to move her to more remote turf. But Agnes resisted so formidably that — in desperation — he wrote a letter of resignation to Mr King. Fortunately for External and the nation, Mr Robertson was persuaded not to send it and, to this day, his extraordinary letter reposes in the Department's capacious files.

During World War II a new and young civil servant, Jules Léger, was transferred from a wartime agency in Ottawa to External. On the due date, he cleared out his old office in the morning and reported in to the East Block by lunch-time. The redoubtable Agnes docked him his first day's pay for failing to start work by 9:00 a.m. Notwithstanding this bad start, he went on to become deputy minister of the Department and then governor general of Canada.

Although Agnes's personal horizon was confined mainly to Ottawa and Chesterville, the reach of her frugality extended far beyond the Ottawa Valley and was felt throughout the whole of the far-flung Canadian foreign service. When young George Ignatieff, who was later to become ambassador to the UN and NATO and chancellor of the University of Toronto, went out on his first posting as an impoverished third secretary to Canada House in London, Agnes arbitrarily decided that he need not be paid the customary living allowance — a paltry enough figure — devised incomprehensibly, Externalites believed, by evil genii at the Dominion Bureau of Statistics. Agnes's diktat prevailed, and required no less than the personal intervention of High Commissioner Vincent Massey to overcome.

When D'Arcy McGreer, with five stepchildren, was appointed to the Canadian Embassy in Tokyo, the ubiquitous Agnes — who had known him earlier when he was a bachelor — became appalled at the thought of the expense that such a move would entail. So she simply cut the travel allowance for the stepchildren in half. That diktat, too, prevailed.

Mike Pearson also felt her sting. At the height of Hitler's buzz-bombing of London during World War II, he wrote a moving report from Canada House describing the havoc

wrought and the dislocation suffered by millions in the British capital — including the staff at Canada House. Agnes decided that, since our people in London could not undertake normal representation functions in such hazardous conditions, she would cut their representation allowances. This moved Mr Pearson to write, in a letter to Norman Robertson:

Thursday: Air-raid shelter for 1½ hours during day.
Friday: Suburban station next to mine hit by bomb
             during evening.
Saturday: Cable from External: "Your allowances are
             cut by 10%."
Sunday: Cable from External (after a heavy night's
             bombing): "You are all much on our minds."
P.S.:   Please get us out of your minds. We don't
             want another cut.

When External officers are appointed to a post abroad, they are issued a new, diplomatic, red-coloured passport indicating their post and rank, and they have to turn it in when they return to Ottawa. For some odd reason known only to herself, Agnes would get possession of the new passports; then, regardless of the hour (usually late at night) or the rigours of Ottawa's Siberian winters, she would go downtown to the old Union Station to hand a departing officer his new red diplomatic passport, just as he was boarding the train for Halifax or Vancouver and the Great Beyond.

On occasion, Miss McCloskey's penuriousness had serious foreign policy implications: for example, for the status of our first diplomatic mission in Havana.

With Canadian Missions in Europe closing as a result of Hitler's conquests, Mr King came round to the view that our representation should be extended in Latin America to counter Axis influence in the Western Hemisphere, and to enlist Latin American support for the Allied cause.

Canadian Missions were opened in Argentina, Brazil and Chile, and Cuba was to follow. To head our Mission in Havana, Mr King chose Montreal businessman Emile Vaillancourt who, not coincidentally, had been instrumental in having Emil Ludwig's biography of the prime minister published in French.

But Mr Vaillancourt was unhappy when he learned that the new Mission would be designated only as "Legation," not "Embassy," which meant that he would have the lower rank of minister and not ambassador. If we were seeking to exert influence in Cuba, he remonstrated, this would be an unnecessary and counterproductive handicap; furthermore, since he wasn't seeking any extra perks, designating the new Mission in Havana an embassy and him ambassador wouldn't cost the taxpayer a single additional penny.

This sounded quite reasonable to Hugh Keenleyside and Arthur Menzies in External's Third Political Division, whose fiefdom was the entire Western Hemisphere; but Agnes settled the matter herself by decreeing that, since a supply of "Canadian Legation, Havana" stationery had already been ordered, External should buy no more. And so the new Mission in Havana started life as a legation. Thus was Canada's New Hemispheric Policy implemented.

I can appreciate Mr Vaillancourt's concern because, when I received my first head-of-post appointment, a quarter century later and after legations had gone out of style, it was not as ambassador but as chargé d'affaires, in Montevideo. Although I remonstrated no less vigorously than Mr Vaillancourt to be designated ambassador, I must confess that my concern was not with the local pecking order in Uruguay but with something quite different: the plight that would face my mother, in her eighties, at the Baycrest Home in Toronto. There she would be, with the other ladies proudly opening their mail "from my son, the doctor," or "from my daughter, the Judge," or "from my nephew, the Professor" — you know how it is with Jewish parents anxious to glory in the learned accomplishments of their offspring. The ladies at Baycrest wouldn't have the vaguest idea of what mother meant if she showed them a letter "from my son, the chargé." Fortunately she lived long enough to upstage her companions with letters, bearing exotic stamps, "from my son, the Ambassador," and I'm sure she revelled in it.

During the war Agnes's autocratic, pecuniary regime was creating such problems throughout the East Block and other buildings in which we were scattered — the Daly, Coleman and Post Office buildings, and the Langevin Block — that she was persuaded to accept a flattering promotion — to be

Canada's first female consul, in New York. When the news of her move from the seat of power reached our legation in Washington, Mr Pearson noted in his diary that it overshadowed all that day's war news: "Even the advance of the Eighth Army had to take second place."

Once installed in New York, Agnes began feuding with the consul general, Hugh Day Scully of Toronto, and for most of her stay they hardly spoke to each other. (I often had to serve diplomatically as their "go-between" — although not as between lovers.) To remove Agnes from New York, the Department sent her on External's first inspection trip of posts abroad, and she then retired.

"Public Service" to the core, mindful of the need for efficiency in government, overzealous and sometimes misguided in applying Regulations, Agnes McCloskey was nevertheless a loyal and dedicated person, kindly of heart and privately helpful to colleagues in difficulties or wounded by her austerities.

Travel and
Removal

With the passing of Agnes McCloskey from our midst, it should not be assumed that the penny-pinching proclivities of External also vanished. For example, there grew up the vexing question of air travel.

In earlier if not more leisurely days, foreign service officers were usually fortunate enough to go to a foreign posting aboard a luxurious transatlantic Cunarder or on the French or Italian Line. Or, if they were going overland, then they would travel on the Trans-Siberian, the Orient Express or the Atchison, Topeka and Santa Fe. I may have been one of the last Canadian foreign service officers to travel *en poste* by surface when, transferred in 1969 from the United Nations to Montevideo, we sailed on a Grace liner from New York through the Panama Canal, with stops all the way down the west coast of South America to Valparaiso, then underwent a hair-raising crossing of 12,000-foot Andes on a narrow-gauge railway from Santiago, Chile, to Mendoza in Argentina, crossed the pampas in a train that must have seen service in the era of Florence Nightingale, sailed by ferry across the Rio de la Plata to Uruguay, and were picked up by embassy stationwagon for the final forty-mile drive to our new post. The whole journey, with three-day stopovers in Santiago and

Buenos Aires, took exactly one month; it would have taken about eighteen hours to fly from New York to Montevideo.

When air travel completely superseded such leisurely surface journeys because it had indeed become more economical, a Great Debate ensued in External Affairs — and intermittently still goes on — over flying by first class or economy. When economy won the day, the argument was made that while Heads of Mission should travel economy on routine business, they should be allowed to fly first class when travelling by air to take up a new post; it would be *infra dig* for a newly appointed ambassador to emerge from the economy exit at the rear of the plane, when it landed at Kinshasa or Kuala Lumpur, where the local chief of protocol, the Canadian Embassy staff and Commonwealth colleagues-to-be would all be gathered to greet him or her on the tarmac at the first-class exit — at the front of the plane.

This argument gathered strength when reports reached Ottawa of a minor fiasco that befell our then-ambassador to the United States, Marcel Cadieux. He had accepted an invitation to fly down to a large Florida city for a region-wide celebration of Canada Day, which the state authorities were supporting enthusiastically. To greet Marcel on his arrival, the Floridians had brought out to the airport a Marine band together with school officials and state and civic dignitaries, who were mustered on the tarmac at the first-class exit of the incoming plane. The flight was booked to capacity, and by the time Marcel managed to emerge from the economy exit and push his way to the front, the greeters — assuming he had missed his flight — had dispersed and were heading back to town.

Notwithstanding such unpleasantries, the hard-nosed boys in Treasury remained unpersuaded by the Department's pleas about denigration. However, some bright soul in External thought up an ingenious compromise, which our imaginative, New Brunswicker under-secretary, Ed Ritchie, approved. Going out to take a new post , our distinguished ambassadors would indeed continue to fly economy — from

Ottawa right up to the last stop before arrival. At that last stop they would shift into first class, and thus be able to emerge at their destination from the proper door and into the waiting arms of the local chief of protocol.

If Crenia and I were about the last to get a fine sea voyage to take up my head-of-post assignment in Montevideo, we were probably the first to perform this new, quick-change, air travel act, on the occasion of my appointment in 1970 as ambassador to Colombia and Ecuador. We flew economy from Ottawa to Toronto to Mexico (for some Spanish language immersion) and thence to Panama, in the same low (economy-class) estate. In Panama, to the surprise of Aerolineas Argentinas officials, we made our sly little shift from economy into first class, enabling us on arrival in Bogota to step out of the front door to receive welcoming *abrazos* from the Colombian *jefe de protocolo*. No one, not even the welcoming Canadian Embassy group, was any the wiser for the sleight-of-hand that made our auspicious "first-class" arrival possible.

On that comfortable last leg of the flight in 'first', from Panama to Bogota, I mused about how Agnes McCloskey in her day might have adapted this change-from-economy-to-first stratagem to steamship and railway travel. Would our new ambassador to Rome, travelling steerage on the *Cristoforo Colombo*, slip up with his steamer trunks to the first-class promenade deck at Nice, or wait until he spotted Vesuvius in the Bay of Naples? Would our new ambassador to Athens, munching a cold, brown-bagged sandwich in the day coach of the Orient Express, lug his bags up to the club car at Skoplje, or wait for Sofia? If we opened a consulate in Vladivostok, would our appointee make his artful little move into first class on the Trans-Siberian at Omsk, Tomsk or Ussuriysk?

These musings led me to recall how my opposite number at the British Embassy in Dublin had travelled *en poste* to take up his new assignment to Ireland. He was a keen sailor, and succeeded in persuading the ogres in Whitehall that they would save sterling by allowing him to sail his 36-foot sloop, with wife, children, dogs and baggage, from Plymouth Rock to the Liffey quays. What pleased him most, when he related this to me, was the hard time he must have given those Treasury types in adapting his *sui generis* travel claim to existing regulations.

Lest you think these examples of External Affairs' concern for the taxpayer's dollar a little far-fetched, let me cite one more, which for security reasons will have to be fudged ever so slightly, but which by no means is apocryphal.

In the early '70s, when aerial highjacking was endemic in Latin America, one of our diplomatic couriers was making the run to deliver diplomatic bags to a number of Canadian embassies in South America. (External's couriers are provided with two first-class, adjoining seats; they place their bags, from which they must not become separated, on one seat and occupy the other.)

As our courier's plane entered Latin American air space, terrorists surfaced from among the passengers, overcame the crew and ordered the plane to land at a nearby airport. There, the highjackers allowed the passengers to go free while they negotiated their demands by radio with the tower. Our courier picked up the diplomatic bags to leave with the other passengers, but the highjackers told him to open the bags. He wouldn't. They told him to leave them behind. He wouldn't. And in the best External tradition, he remained with his bags, on the plane.

While negotiations between the highjackers and the tower dragged on, the local authorities managed to bring up a special tactical unit, which stormed the plane. Bursting in one door with a hose, they shot fire-extinguishing foam into the interior to smother flames from any explosions, dousing our courier.

The operation was successful; the crew and our valiant but soggy courier were freed; and after a quick airport dry-cleaning job on his suit, he continued on his appointed rounds. At the next capital, a clerk from the Canadian

Embassy met him to pick up the diplomatic bags for that post, and handed him telegrams from the minister and under-secretary in Ottawa commending him for devotion to the service over and above the call of duty.

When he got back to Ottawa, he put in his regular travel-expense claim, including a $2 charge for dry-cleaning one soggy, foam-soaked suit. It was turned down — on the grounds that he hadn't been absent from Ottawa the required number of hours when the dry-cleaning took place.

The members of our embassy in Tehran, whose valour in protecting their American colleagues and then spiriting them to safety, received wide acclaim from the prime minister and the United States president down. They found that their claims, however, for personal effects they had to leave behind when they made their exit, were cut by two-thirds through Treasury regulations.

Public – and
Not-So-Public –
Affairs

Having served two rather strenuous tours of duty as External's spokesman and head of the press office — once in the early '50s and again in the early '60s — I thought I knew a fair amount about how to deal with the press and allied media. But when George Cowley told me what he had to do to surmount a problem in press relations that confronted him in the mid-'60s, I realized that there is always something more to be learned in plying this difficult trade.

Cowley was a junior officer in the Department's Commonwealth division at the time, and one of his duties was to serve as Australian desk officer. At that time Paul Martin was our secretary of state for external affairs and, while attending a session of the United Nations General Assembly in New York, he had held some discussions with Australian External Affairs Minister Paul Hasluck. Mr Martin urged Mr Hasluck to make a visit to Ottawa before returning to Canberra. Mr Hasluck agreed.

A few days later Mr and Mrs Hasluck, together with a sallow individual who served as the Australian minister's confidential messenger and valet, flew from New York to Ottawa where, at Uplands Airport, George Cowley had assembled a welcoming party of high-level functionaries.

But, as often happens in Ottawa, a considerable fog had moved in and the official greeters could hear the invisible plane circling the airport for a while and then flying away.

Learning that the plane was headed for Montreal's Dorval Airport, Cowley prevailed upon the Department of National Defence to provide a car and driver for the Hasluck party's two-hour drive back to Ottawa. The driver was instructed to bring the Haslucks to the VIP (west) entrance to the Chateau Laurier Hotel, and young Cowley and his cohorts took up positions there.

But the Army driver was not blessed with a sense of our capital's geography and got lost in the environs of Ottawa. He finally made it to the centre of town and the Chateau Laurier Hotel, where he deposited the Hasluck party, not at the prestigious, west entrance, but at the dingy, east door. That happens to be a service entrance to the bowels of the hotel, and without a doorman in sight.

There, the Haslucks and their sallow aide found themselves negotiating a cellar catwalk, heavy with all their luggage, through the boiler room, where Mrs Hasluck lost the heel of one shoe. The dust and vapour from the Chateau's odoriferous furnaces did little to improve their first impressions of Canada's capital. By the time the driver realized that they had used the wrong door and led them back outside and around to the west entrance, Cowley's welcomers had drifted away leaving only him — a junior third secretary — to welcome Australia's minister of external affairs and his wife, sprinkled with the Chateau's soot and clutching detached clothing.

As planned, next morning Mr Hasluck went over to Mr Martin's office for an exchange of views, but our Minister was delayed in a protracted cabinet meeting. While Mr Hasluck was waiting, his valet showed up with a pair of cufflinks that had been mislaid. As he started to leave, in walked Mr Martin, who embraced the valet with, "Oh, so good to see you here, Paul."

Thereafter, the visit proceeded uneventfully — that is,

until Mr Hasluck informed Cowley that, before leaving Ottawa the next afternoon, he would be glad to meet with representatives of the Canadian news media. When Cowley sought to set up a press conference for the Australian visitor, he ran into an unexpected problem.

The Gerda Munsinger affair, the sex-and-security drama of the decade, had broken wide open in the House of Commons and it immediately became a national *cause-célèbre*. Every journalist in the nation's capital was glued to his seat in the jam-packed Commons' parliamentary press gallery, riveted on the Question Period unfolding in the House. George Cowley soon found that he could arouse no interest whatsoever in a press conference with an Australian minister for external affairs.

The next day, shortly before the press conference was due to begin, not a single journalist was in sight. Cowley, still brooding over the impending debacle, devised a scheme. He corralled half a dozen junior External colleagues and pressed them to show up with notebooks and pepper Canada's Australian guest with questions on which Cowley would prepare them.

But what about tv? Cowley found that every television crew in town was focussed on Parliament Hill's sex drama, but he rose to this crisis, too. He prevailed on tv network friends who "owed him one" to send over an off-duty crew; they would have cameras grinding away, without film, but with their lights blazing on the unwitting Australian.

But wouldn't the Haslucks be watching the 6 p.m. news to witness the minister's debut on Canadian television? Not to worry, Cowley assured the network and his growing coterie of accomplices: the Haslucks would be winging their way Canberra-ward before the critical hour.

And what about the Australian high commissioner's office in Ottawa? No problem. Cowley would bring those nice Australian chaps in on his dark little secret. They would have to be brought in anyway, since they would recognize the fake reporters at the "press conference."

When Mr Hasluck showed up to meet with representatives of the Canadian press, Cowley's young External colleagues performed admirably, notebooks in hand, peppering the minister with perceptive questions about Australia's relations with countries of the Pacific Rim, South Pacific defence strategy, Chinese representation at the United Nations and the future of Taiwan, and the continuing war in Indochina. One of the " reporters" — junior Third Secretary Peyton Lyon — even showed up with green celluloid eyeshades and shirtsleeves held up with garters, in the best tradition of Ben Hecht and Charles MacArthur's great movie, *Front Page*; Lyon went on to become a professor of diplomacy at Carleton University's Patterson School of International Relations.

The following week Cowley queried Canada's Mission in Canberra on the Hasluck visit, as seen from the Australian end. He was not surprised at Canberra's reply: "The Australian Department of External Affairs had displayed a "curious reticence" on the subject.

A Man
for all Seasons

If Canada elected a Man For All Seasons, for this century, I suspect the choice would unhesitatingly be Lester B. "Mike" Pearson, not only for his extraordinary skills in international diplomacy and the renown he brought Canada as a world statesman, but for his uncanny sense of humour — spontaneous, seemingly irrepressible, and likely to erupt at the most unexpected moments and in the most unlikely situations.

Back in 1961, after he had left the public service and was leading the Liberal Party, he visited his riding of Algoma East. After fielding political questions during a conference with the press, a reporter asked him — Pearson was an avid baseball fan — which team he thought would win the World Series about to commence between the Cincinnati Reds and the New York Yankees.

Unhesitatingly he picked New York, and the reporter asked him why.

"Can you imagine the headlines if I predicted that Cincinnati would win?" Mr Pearson responded. "PEARSON FAVOURS REDS OVER YANKEES."

Later, when his government was suffering a buffeting in the House of Commons, and he was asked what he would

do if the Opposition embarked on some new and horrendous tack, he remarked, "I'll fall off that bridge when I come
to it."

Even more extraordinary was the way Mike Pearson, with
exquisite timing and just the right degree of levity, would
come up with something in the midst of a delicate diplomatic
negotiation. He could relax up-tight participants, get them
laughing instead of glaring at each other and, quite often,
break a deadlock or get over some contentious hump that
was holding up agreement.

When he did this at the United Nations, their crack simultaneous interpreters, used to coping calmly with all manner
of violent outbursts, could scarcely restrain their laughter as
they sought to render Pearson's joke into Chinese, Russian,
or whatever.

Here is a typical example, from a tense session at the
Commonwealth Prime Ministers' Conference in London in
1964, as recalled by Commonwealth Secretary-General
Arnold Smith in his *Stitches in Time*.

The British had been fearing an explosion when the
contentious topic of Southern Rhodesia was to be discussed,
so Commonwealth and Colonial Secretary Duncan Sandys
started with an eloquent speech about Britain's decoloniza-
tion record, giving 700 million people in a score of countries
their independence, which, he noted, Britain had done not
through any lack of power but of her own free will.

This provoked Hastings Banda, whose country, Malawi,
had achieved independence only a few days earlier, to
respond:

"Now come, Mr Chairman, let's be frank with each other.
You British have not been as pig-headed as other imperial-
ists. You have recognized in time what is inevitable and
accepted it gracefully. That is your greatness and we honour
you for it. But…there's been a significant element of persua-
sion, and many of us here have been among the persuaders."

Banda himself had spent thirteen months in a Rhodesian
prison, and he went around the room pointing to new

Commonwealth prime ministers and citing their prison terms — Ghana's Nkrumah, Kenya's Kenyatta, Cyprus's Archbishop Makarios, and he included India's Jawaharlal Nehru, who had just died. "I wanted to make my point frankly," Banda said. "Frankness is the basis of our association."

There was nervous laughter around the room. The atmosphere had become increasingly tense — until Pearson broke in.

He liked being included in "inner circles," he quipped, and one seemed to be forming here, "of prison graduates." His own qualifications for membership were modest: he had been confined to barracks for a week when he was a medical orderly during the First World War; could he not qualify? Everybody laughed, and he had broken the build-up of tension completely.

Himself a product of the manse, Mike Pearson was the last person to be disrespectful of anyone's religion. Thus, a little remark that came unexpectedly from his lips in Ceylon back in 1950 should in no way be considered irreverent.

He had gone to Colombo to attend the First Conference of Commonwealth Foreign Ministers. Such was his reputation by that time that the Ceylonese urged him to stay on after the conference to make a short official visit, of which a highlight was a tour of the ancient Sinhalese capital of Kandy in the hills above Colombo.

There he was taken to the Temple of the Tooth to see the famed tooth of Buddha, an object of veneration shown only on important religious occasions or to only the most distinguished of visitors.

The ceremony involved taking off a succession of seven silver and gold goblet-shaped covers to reveal the historic tooth — which turned out to be extraordinarily large, and yellow with age. When he saw it, and before launching into his respectful words about the great religious contribution of Buddha to Asia and the world since 500 B.C., Mike turned to his Canadian aides — Douglas LePan, Escott Reid and Arthur

Menzies — and whispered: "What a wonderful opportunity for a toothpaste ad."

A Canadian For All Seasons indeed.

Inter-embassy soccer and other games are commonplace today. But Pearson cooked up the grand-daddy of them all back in wartime 1943 while serving at the Canadian Legation in Washington, but that event needs, nay deserves, its own chapter.

Washington

The Sporting Life

It took me forty years to catch up with the facts — found in some extraordinary documents buried away in External's dormant archives — about this episode in Canada-United States diplomatic relations. For reasons that will become clear, the story will not form part of the Department's official history, which External's specialists have been preparing. Since my tales deal with matters somewhat less than official, I have no inhibition in bringing the documents to light, for they reveal a sense of fun and games in contrast to, and perhaps in comic relief from, the cataclysmic wartime events with which these gentlemen were preoccupied.

By a sort of verbal osmosis, some of us who used to toil in External Affairs' early headquarters in the East Block on Parliament Hill would hear a fleeting word about a legendary baseball game alleged to have been played during the World War II years between the Canadian Legation in Washington and the United States Department of State.

This game did, in fact, get some credence around Ottawa because, for one thing, the second-in-command at our legation in Washington at the time was a notoriously avid baseball fan with an irrepressible sense of humour, Mr Lester B. "Mike" Pearson. For another, in those days — when our bilateral problems with the United States were less complex and vexing and we were marching arm-in-arm as Allies in a struggle to the finish against the Axis — there was a happy informality, an easy intimacy, a warmth and friendliness in the professional and personal relationships between the two North American diplomatic communities that just might have made such a baseball game less improbable than it sounds today.

A word about the *dramatis personae*. "Mike" Pearson needs no introduction in these pages. Jack Hickerson was a distinguished officer in the State Department who had previously served at the United States Embassy in Ottawa and in the State Department's bureau of European affairs, which dealt with relations with Canada; in both places, he had won admiration and the personal friendship of our people. The "Hull Hillbillies" were not denizens of the city of Hull, but were State Department officers working under Cordell Hull, the American wartime secretary of state. Other characters will be readily identifiable.

Now let the documents, possibly unique in the annals of Western diplomacy, speak for themselves.

SECRET, CONFIDENTIAL, AND ALMOST IMPORTANT. TO BE DESTROYED BEFORE READING.
The Hon. Theodore Achilles
Department of State
Washington, D.C.
April 20, 1943

Sir:

I have been requested by Their Excellencies, the various Canadian officials now serving in this penal settlement of Washington, to throw at the State Department a challenge to a test of strength or skill on what is, I believe, known as a baseball diamond. This game of baseball is understood to be the national sport of both the United States and Japan, and, though unknown in Canada, it is consistent with the well-known chivalry and generosity of the challengers to offer to participate in this game in preference to one of the more familiar Canadian games, such as snowshoe running, ludo, bull-baiting, and "I spy Dominion status."

Details as to the time, place, and circumstances of the proposed encounter can be left, it is hoped, to the State Department. We would, however, like to submit certain conditions for your consideration, and, if possible, acceptance:

1. It is felt that complete secrecy should be observed about the whole matter; therefore the publicity and press facilities to be given this contest should be those laid down by the United States Government for the forthcoming United Nations Food Conference.

2. Mr John Hickerson should be a member of the State Department team. In view of the fact that we are playing baseball at all and not one of the Canadian sports mentioned above, and also in view of the fact that we propose to use Mr Merchant Mahoney as a base runner, we feel obliged to ask for this concession.

3. The umpires should be the Director General, Office of Civilian Defence, and the Controller of Bits and Pieces of the War Production Board.

4. All wagers on this game are to be in terms of "Unitas" and not of "Bancor."

5. The challenging team shall have the right to call off the game at the end of the first innings if sufficient replacement for the exhausted and the maimed are not available.

6. In all correspondence, the Canadian team shall be referred to as "Les Panzers Canadiens."

7. The locale of the game shall be considered as a combat area, and all those participating shall be eligible for combat medals and the Order of the Purple Heart.

The Canadian Legation awaits in hope and confidence your favourable consideration of this challenge, which, I may add, is sent without the knowledge or approval of either Dr Goebbels or the Canadian-American Permanent Board of Defence.

I have the honour to be,

Sir,

With highest respect,

Your most humble, obedient servant,

L.B. Pearson

The Dishon.
L.B. Pearson
First Base (Very)
Canadian Legation
Washington, D.C.

Sir:

I am directed to acknowledge your discourteous note of today's date and to assure you that it will receive the consideration which it merits. You will be advised in due course of the views of the competent authorities.

Accept, you so and so, the renewed assurances of my moderate consideration.

Very truly yours,

Theodore C. Achilles

Chargé-d'Athlétiques Étrangères

but *not* of the Division of Cultural Relations, (by God).

NOT CONFIDENTIAL BUT UNPRINTABLE,
URGENT AND USELESS
The Dishon.
L.B. Pearson
First Base (Very)
Canadian Legation

Dear Lester:

Having regard for the presumptuous tone of your igno-minious communication of the 29th ult., I have little honor in informing you that the State Department Team (Hull Hillbillies) accepts the challenge of his Britannic Majesty's representatives for Canada in Washington, Georgetown, and Falls Church, under the following conditions which, it is hoped, need not be formalized in an Exchange of Notes. (If, however, you won't play without such an exchange, it is proposed that the necessary exchange or exchanges be exchanged at the official discount rate prescribed by the Foreign Exchange Control Board.)

1. The game to be baseball — softball, in fact, in consideration of the softness of the Canadian team — and to last three innings or until your team is unable to take the field, whichever comes first. Under no circumstances, however, shall Les Panzers Canadiens use hockey sticks, or lacrosse sticks. (Crutches, however, will be permitted for purposes of locomotion only.)

2. The game to be under the control, when convenient to the Hull Hillbillies, of two umpires, who will be under no obligation to extend unconditional most-favored-nation treatment. Instead of the persons so ungraciously nominated in your note under reference, it is proposed that the said umpires shall be selected from a panel to be composed of high ranking officers of Northwest Airlines and farmers from Aroostook County, Maine. Representatives of other American airlines whose operations in Canada have not yet come to the attention of the Canadian authorities may, however, qualify if they can evade the terms of an overall master agreement between the two Governments.

3. The umpires to have sole, not concurrent, jurisdiction over all crimes including murder, manslaughter and rape. In general, the "knock for knock" policy will prevail although due regard may be had for the principle of "hot pursuit." "Wildcatting," however, is not to be permitted save in an area to be bounded by the 49th parallel, Hudson's Bay, the Alaskan boundary, the Arctic and Pacific Oceans and by line A–B (if Canada can find it).

4. The teams to be costumed and disarrayed as follows:
The Hull Hillbillies — Tuxedos
Les Panzers Canadiens — Prince Alberts (with or without Medicine Hat).
5. The Hull Hillbillies, out of sympathy for the Canadian manpower problem, to be composed exclusively of gentlemen from the Division of European Affairs speaking the national language of the United States and Les Panzers Canadiens to be bilingual representatives of the Dominion, including not less than:

One Protestant from Quebec
One Catholic from Ontario
One nephew of Sir Wilfrid Laurier
One niece of Sir John A. Macdonald
One exponent of Maritime Grievances
One member of the Cooperative Commonwealth Confederation who shall be a Rhodes Scholar
One member of the Department of External Affairs who shall not be a Rhodes Scholar
One member of the Canadian Delegation concerning whom there is no dossier in the files of the Royal Canadian Mounted Police.

It is, of course, understood, stipulated and insisted upon that all members of the Canadian team shall be in favour of full Dominion status, although, if it is so desired, this Government will interpose no objection to the nomination as batboy (not batman) of a representative of the Colonial Office.

It is agreed that complete secrecy shall be observed and to that end the counter proposal is made that full details should be placed in the hands of the Wartime Information Board of Canada. The suggestion that these representatives of the press should be entertained at the Homestead, is, however, indignantly, irrevocably and irresolutely rejected unless Mr Grierson is prepared to accept conditions of reverse Lend Lease. Refreshments will, however, be served by the Bronfman brothers.

I am further authorized to inform you that Mr John Hickerson, the Texas Terror, shall indeed be a member of the State Department team and that, out of special consideration for Les Panzers Canadiens, he has consented to participate without his distinguished colleagues on the Permanent Joint Board of Defense. Mr Hickerson's wagers will be in Confederate currency, not Unitas; accordingly, Mr Merchant Mahoney may, if he can, place bets in terms of Social Credit.

The combat area in which this stupendous struggle is to take place, as well as the date and time, shall, it is suggested, be the subject of discussions between your assistant, Mr Magann, and my assistant, Mr Parsons, inasmuch as they are already quite used to arguing with each other.

Accept, my dear Lester, what consideration I have left.
Very truly yours,
Theodore C. Achilles
Chargé-d'Athlétiques Étrangères

The game — following hard on the heels of this not-so-diplomatic exchange — apparently did take place, and facts and fiction — not always separated — gradually made their way to Ottawa. According to one legend, if a Canadian made it to first base, a State-Department junior would be standing in the first base coaching box to hand him a martini from a loaded tray. If an American made it to first base, a Canadian Legation slavey similarly would be there to accord him similar treatment. And for anyone on either team who managed to make it to third, the process would be repeated, presumably in order to recharge the batteries for the hoped-for assault on home plate: a far cry from the World Series!

In the days and weeks after the game, the following "Notes" were despatched.

Unnumbered
Secretary of State
for External Affairs
Ottawa, Canada
June 25, 1943

Sir:

I have the honour to enclose herewith copies of secret and
insulting correspondence between the Department of
State and this Legation regarding a challenge issued by
the latter for a game of baseball between "Les Panzers
Canadiens" of the Legation and the "Hull Hillbillies" of
the State Department. It is hoped that this correspondence can be carefully considered by those in the Department who are — and have been since 1927 — working on
regulations regarding the correct form and style to be
used in diplomatic communications between governments. The Legation considers these exchanges to be mod-

els of their kind and have been informed that the feeling in
the State Department supports this view.

The game in question, after many delays due to heat,
work, and the general disinclination to indulge in any form
of unnecessary activity, was finally played Wednesday
evening of this week on the campus of Georgetown University, before a large, enthusiastic, partisan, and perspiring
audience.

The Canadian team, all of whom are hereby mentioned
in despatches and who, it is hoped, will receive suitable
recognition in the forthcoming Honours List, which, it is
understood, will be issued on the 12th of July, consisted of
practically every member of the Legation Staff, together
with three members of other Canadian Government
offices in Washington, who, in recognition of their long
and effective service in those offices, were made honorary
Attachés of the Legation for the day.

The State Department team, violently led by Mr John
Hickerson and under the field captaincy of that redoubtable athlete, Mr James Bonbridge, suffered a catastrophic
Pearl Harbor in the first innings, when Les Panzers
scored ten runs before they declared the innings closed.
However, the Americans, undaunted, rushed in reinforce-
ments, and, with the able assistance of the sportsmanlike
Canadian team, who withdrew their best pitcher and sub-
stituted for him the aged and inefficient Mr Pearson, were
able to creep up until they were within striking distance of
Les Panzers.

It would, of course, have been inappropriate if the Legation had won; it would have been humiliating if it had lost.
With the score 17-13 in favour of the Legation and two out
in the 9th, it appeared that our desire to ensure perma-
nently friendly relations with the State Department
might not be achieved. However, four errors in quick succession, and a tremendous, but accidental three-base hit
by Mr Hickerson permitted four runs to be scored. The
game thereby ended happily for all concerned, who imme-

diately adjourned to the residence of Mr Theodore
Achillies, where hospitality was accepted and aching mus-
cles assuaged. The final score 17–17 will, it is hoped, be
interpreted as the most striking evidence yet submitted of
the diplomatic skill of the officers of the Legation.
I have the honour to be, Sir,
Your obedient servant,
L.B. Pearson

No. Blank
The Canadian Minister to the United States
Canadian Legation
Washington, D.C.
July 17, 1943

Sir:

I regret that it is my duty to acknowledge your unnumbered despatch of June 25, 1943, and attachments, in
which you reported certain of the more printable details of
a recent encounter between representatives of the Legation and the United States Department of State in a game
described, with your habitual inaccuracy, as "baseball."
Fortunately, and as usual, we have been able to supple-
ment and correct the material supplied in your despatch
under reference by information received through more
responsible channels. Eminent among these have been Mr
Drew Pearson, Colonel Robert MacCormick, Informed
Circles in Washington and Mr Lewis Clark. (In the latter
case an acknowledgment giving the view of the Canadian
Government was demanded by 3 p.m. (Early Washington
Time) on the day of receipt.)

   It would be a difficult and, of course, a useless task to
cover in one despatch all the points at which the Legation
was in error in the correspondence under reference.

   Why, for example, was no protest made in relation to
the name selected by the representatives of the State
Department? The fact that Mr John Hickerson, Mr

Graham Parsons and other Hillbillies were customarily to be found within the environs of the municipality located north of the Ottawa River during the time they were laughingly referred to as being *en poste* in the Canadian capital should not have been accepted as justification for the adoption of the name of a Canadian city to describe a group of Giraudists and Ottonians.

Your despatch, moreover, gave no indication of the means employed to remove the Americans from bases once occupation had been achieved. Surely a significant accomplishment of this kind was worthy of detailed report. It is the omission of Vital information of this kind that has created the impression in the American Division of the Department that reports from Washington are edited to avoid All the News That's Fit to Print.

Certain textual aberrations should also be brought to your attention. In the second paragraph of your despatch you referred to the "general disinclination" of members of the Legation staff "to indulge in any form of unnecessary activity." "Unnecessary" is surely unnecessary.

In the fourth paragraph you refer to the "first innings." Surely even a team of Rhodes Scholars, led by a pensioned player of lacrosse, should know that "innings" is cricket but baseball is "inning." In baseball the singular is always used, and never, I should judge, with more justification than in the present instance.

I observe that you omit all reference to the aluminum bat with which I understand the Legation team was supplied by grateful representatives of a distinguished Canadian political party. Nor do I find any comment on the Land-Luce movement which certain members of the State Department team are reported to have initiated with a view to distracting the attention of the Canadian players. A message on this subject was received by our Code Room — *en clair*.

In the final paragraph you wrote "Yesterday the State Department was temporarily converted into an emergency hospital, but the Legation functioned in its usual smooth and efficient manner." May I suggest that the truth would have been macerated sufficiently to meet your usual standards if the last phrase of this sentence were altered to read "and the Legation functioned period."

Your explanation of the failure of the Canadian team to win the game is neither plausible nor convincing and varies in many particulars from the accounts given by Mr Hickerson to the members of the Permanent Joint Board on Defence, the Soviet airman at Fairbanks, the United States contractors on the Alaska Highway, the Sourdoughs of Skagway and Whitehorse, and certain Army nurses encountered at various points on his recent tour of Western America. These accounts, however, varying as they did with the alleged position of the sun in relation to the yardarm, were often as incredible as your own. Perhaps under the circumstances it would be as well to allow the matter to rest. This objective can, of course, be most effectively achieved by referring it to the Department of State with a request for an early and intelligible expression of views. Such reference is hereby authorized.

I have the honour to be, Sir,
Your obedient servant,
H.L. Keenleyside

PS. It is with some regret that I feel compelled to point out that attendance at the alleged baseball game — or some other cause — has made it impossible for the officers of the Legation to report to this Department on the extinction of five and the creation of seventeen new Boards or other major agencies of Government which took place in Washington during the hours in which the said game was in progress. You will undoubtedly wish to take this fact into account when considering further activities of a sportive nature.

When the Expos and the Blue Jays meet each year in midseason to play the Pearson Cup exhibition game, few spectators — or players for that matter — will know anything about the person for whom the trophy is named. And almost certainly none will know of that earlier game that Mr Pearson organized in the interest of diplomacy — and good times.

That Unguarded Frontier

As World War II was reaching its climax in the spring of 1945, news of the death of the great wartime president of the United States, Franklin Delano Roosevelt, reverberated around the world. In many capitals, the first thought of Canadian diplomats was to make a call at the local American Embassy to express sympathy to their American colleagues. In Rio de Janeiro, then the capital of Brazil, the call was made by the Canadian ambassador, accompanied by an old friend and colleague of mine in earlier years, Second Secretary Benjamin Rogers. The American ambassador on whom they called was Mr Adolf A. Berle, Jr who, reminiscing about his experiences with Canada during the war, told his Canadian visitors a couple of stories that might add a footnote to the lighter side of Canada-United States relations.

When World War II first broke out in 1939, the hostilities were all in Europe, and the United States remained neutral. Mr Berle, who had been prominent in academic life, was then in the high position in Washington of assistant secretary of state. It fell to him to prepare a draft of the proclamation that was to be issued by the United States under its Neutrality Act. In his draft, he had to list the countries that were then at

100

war in its first days, and he listed Canada as a belligerent, together with the other British Dominions.

Mr Berle took his draft to the White House to secure presidential approval. President Roosevelt read the draft over and then asked Berle his reasons for including Canada among the nations already at war.

Mr Berle gave the president two reasons for including Canada, one legal, the other political. In the first place, he said, a Canadian attorney general had expressed the opinion that if Great Britain were at war, Canada *ipso facto* would be at war. In the second place, he supposed that the United States government would not wish to do anything that might make the United Kingdom's position more difficult at such a critical time; if the United States listed Canada as a neutral, would this not be taking a position on a delicate aspect of intra-Commonwealth relations that might add to Britain's grave problems at the very outset of war? No such question arose regarding the other Dominions, since they had all already declared war or had stated that they were bound by the United Kingdom's declaration of war.

After listening to these explanations from his assistant secretary of state, Mr Roosevelt pondered for a moment and then put in a telephone call to Ottawa to speak with his great friend Prime Minister Mackenzie King, who at that time also served as his own secretary of state for external affairs.

As Mr Berle recalled to his Canadian visitors in Rio de Janeiro, the president's words to Mr King went somewhat as follows: "They seem to think down here in Washington that Canada is already at war. I have told them that I doubt it, and that's why I am calling. You, Mr prime minister, are the person who should know." Mr King told the president that the question of Canada's entry into the war would be decided by the Canadian Parliament, which he had summoned to meet within the next few days to take a vote on this very question.

When he received Mr King's reply, President Roosevelt issued the appropriate instructions and then said to his assistant secretary of state: "Whenever you have to choose between Ottawa and London, don't forget that Ottawa is a lot nearer to the USA."

A few months later, Mr Berle told a story that illustrates another dimension of Canada-United States relations. As assistant secretary at the State Department in Washington, he had to go to Ottawa on some official business, and he took the overnight train from New York to Montreal.

At the last stop before arriving at the border, a Canadian Customs and Immigration official boarded the train and began his duties. When he reached Berle and asked the customary questions, Berle showed his official passport and said he was going to Ottawa to confer with members of the Canadian government. The Immigration officer wished him a pleasant journey and expressed the hope that his visit to Ottawa would be successful.

Three nights later, on the way back to New York, at the last stop in Canada before crossing the border, a pair of men wearing U.S. Customs and Immigration hats boarded the train and began to question the passengers. When they reached Berle he showed them his official United States passport and said that he had been in Ottawa for a couple of days on official business. One of the Immigration officers wished him a pleasant journey and expressed the hope that his visit to Ottawa had been successful.

"Say, haven't I seen you before?" Berle asked. "Weren't you the person that examined me the other day when I was on my way to Ottawa?"

"You're absolutely right, sir. You see, we work pretty closely with our opposite numbers down here. We try, when it's necessary, to cover each other off. The American Immigration man's wife is having a baby and I'm covering for him tonight. We do this for each other at the border."

Latin America

Ham-Fisted
at High Altitude

Whenever I read in the newspapers that another head of state or head of government is going to visit Ottawa, and when I reflect on all the arrangements that have to be made and all the flaps that can occur, my mind goes back to the summer of 1973 when M. Nicolai Ceausescu, president of the State Council of Romania, and Mme Ceausescu made a state visit to Ecuador, accompanied by their nineteen-year-old son and twenty-one-year-old daughter, three high-ranking cabinet ministers, ten senior government officials, several officials of the Romanian Communist Party, a contingent of security guards, a food-taster, a tailor, and a barber/hairdresser — a total entourage of eighty-one.

At that time, President Ceausescu had achieved the reputation of having a greater degree of flexibility in foreign policy than any of his neighbours in the Soviet-dominated Eastern European bloc. If, for that reason, the Ecuadorians had any illusions that the Romanians would be less demanding of their hosts, they were in for a rude shock. I was Canadian ambassador to Colombia at the time, accredited also to Ecuador, and I had to go down to its capital, Quito, on business just as the Romanians were leaving. Everyone in town seemed to be talking about them — and nothing else.

To begin with, I learned that it was the Romanians who had pressed for the visit. The Ecuadorians had finally agreed in view of their growing discoveries of oil, the completion of the trans-Andean pipeline, and the possibility of discussing petroleum matters with an important European producer.

The first wrangle began — long before the guests arrived — over accommodation. The local practice was to house distinguished visitors in the Hotel Intercontinental Quito, probably the most spectacularly located hotel in all Latin America, with breathtaking views of tropical valleys and the Andes, including three perpetually snow-covered, extinct volcanoes. And it was a well-appointed, well-run establishment indeed.

However, an advance party from Bucharest insisted that their president should be housed in a private villa. So the hosts went to some trouble to secure one, but they could not find anyone with the appropriately appointed mansion who would be willing to give it up for the required time.

To the Ecuadorians' surprise, the advance party said they had found one themselves. But it would need some fixing up, to the tune of around $7,000 — a large sum in the local currency in pre-inflation 1973. To this, the Ecuadorians dug in their heels; the house for which the Romanians had been pushing, incidentally, happened to be the property of a leading member of the local Communist Party.

At this impasse, the advance party finally agreed that the Ceausescus be housed in the Intercontinental's presidential suite. But they insisted on different furniture. The hosts reluctantly agreed, assuming in their bewilderment that this unusual change was requested because of Romanian concern about bugging devices.

But the advance party then insisted that the colour scheme in the presidential suite would not suit the Ceausescus — and the astonished Ecuadorians consented to a quite-unneeded paint job. And just before the arrival, the advance party insisted that the curtains be changed — to achieve greater harmony of surroundings.

For visits of this kind, it is the long-established, internationally accepted practice for the host country to pay for the accommodation and hospitality it offers, and for the guests to pay for a celebratory function in reciprocation. Ecuadorian President Rodriguez Lara would offer, among other things, a state banquet, and the Romanians would offer a buffet dinner. But the Romanians wanted their hosts to pay for the buffet dinner — at which the Ecuadorians again had to dig in their heels. They said that if their visitors wished to omit the return hospitality it would be quite all right — and if not, they would, as is customary, have to pay for it.

With such contentious preliminaries, it was perhaps remarkable that the visit actually took place. But it did, and the contretemps continued for the duration.

When the Ecuadorian chief of protocol dropped in to the ministry's kitchen to see how preparations were going for the luncheon that his foreign minister would be tending, he was forcible ejected by some Romanians who insisted that *they* would be preparing the food. After President Rodriguez Lara's wife, ill in hospital, sent Mme Ceausescu a beautiful gold bracelet and necklace as a gift, one can imagine her astonishment at receiving — in flower-prolific Ecuador — a bouquet of three carnations in return. (Whenever I checked into the Intercontinental Quito, I would find a dozen carnations or orchids in my room, courtesy of the management. The sending of three carnations in Ecuador, especially in the gift-exchanging context, could be interpreted only as a studied insult.)

In any event, because of the illness of the president's wife, the wife of Ecuador's foreign minister gave a tea for Mme Ceausescu to meet the wives of cabinet ministers. Mme C. arrived, drank half a cup of tea, said she was tired — which the ladies assumed would be due to Quito's 9,200-foot altitude — but she then embarked on a strenuous sightseeing tour.

For another luncheon being offered by the Ecuadorian foreign minister, the chief of protocol dropped by the Inter-

continental Hotel to pick up and escort President Ceausescu.
But without any warning, the president said he didn't want
to go and would be grateful if the lunch were cancelled. To
this the chief of protocol responded that the lunch would go
on as planned, since his minister would not wish to embar-
rass the other guests, and that if the president did not wish to
attend, the Ecuadorian government would consider the visit
to be at an end.

Despite these vicissitudes — making one wonder why on
earth these things are ever undertaken in the first place —
the state visit went on, although the nightmares were by no
means concluded.

The two presidents had fixed a time for a ceremonial
signing of a Joint Declaration. Prominent guests had been
invited to watch, the press would be on hand, and radio and
tv time had been booked with satellite feeds and all the other
paraphernalia of modern telecommunications required to
draw the attention of the outside world to the great event
unfolding in this isolated capital in the high Andes.

As the agreed time drew near, M. Ceausescu wanted to
keep the Ecuadorian president and his distinguished guests
waiting an hour or so — because he wanted to receive a local
Communist Party delegation in his hotel. The way the
Ecuadorians fielded this one was to say that that would be
quite all right, but that there would be no Joint Declaration if
the president of Romania did not keep his appointment with
the president of Ecuador, on time.

Then there was the little matter of M. Ceausescu taking it
upon himself to invite two Communist Party leaders from
each Ecuadorian province to meet him — not in his hotel
suite but in the Presidential Palace. As this was a quite extra-
curricular, *ad hoc*, affair, the Ecuadorians handled it by simply refusing the invitees entry to the palace.

For President Rodriguez Lara's state dinner, the
Ceausescus insisted that their children be seated above the
members of the Ecuadorian cabinet and the diplomatic
corps. The beleaguered chief of protocol had to point out

that such precedence would apply only to princes in direct line of heredity; the Ceausescus' request would violate the protocol of Ecuador, which was embodied in Ecuadorian law, and this could not be broken to accommodate the whims of the president of the Socialist Republic of Romania.

The locals then thought up a way to solve this little problem: they would invite President Rodriguez Lara's eldest son and seat him with the Ceausescu offspring. But the Romanian socialist children weren't having any of this. They simply did not attend the banquet.

The hosts were distressed to find that each meal they tendered was delayed by Romanian agents creating havoc in the kitchens and insisting on tasting all dishes to be placed before their president. Then at *their* return meal — the Romanians' buffet dinner at the Hotel Intercontinental Quito — they insisted on mixing all the drinks. When the Mexican and Uruguayan ambassadors sat down during cocktails for a chat, Romanian security guards ordered them to stand up: no one was to sit down except the presidential party. The Japanese ambassador, on arriving, went directly to the bar rather than wait for a drink to be served him, and he was refused by the Romanian security-guard/bartender. The Ecuadorian guests and the diplomatic corps observed that the Romanian entourage — the hosts — were served different, and better, food.

And, finally, as if to top off this circus of incivility: with some reluctance, the Ecuadorians agreed that President Ceausescu would pay a visit to the Central University, make a speech and receive an honorary degree. The hosts — and listeners — were taken aback not so much by the communist clichés in his speech as by its insulting and vitriolic tone, by his snide comments on Ecuador's "revolution," and by his scathing reference to Ecuador's attitude to Allende's socialist government in Chile.

One Ecuadorian cabinet minister said that he had never negotiated with such an ill-mannered group of foreigners; he found his Romanian opposite number so rude and insulting that he refused to attend the Romanian reception for the Ecuadorian president or the farewell at the airport.

On returning to Bogota, I learned that similar shenanigans had gone on during the Romanian visit there, and in Caracas, too. The Latin Americans viewed these surprising events more in puzzlement than in anger, unable to comprehend how an allegedly enlightened Communist leader, with his reputation for having achieved a more flexible foreign policy that the USSR permitted other states in its Eastern European orbit, could indulge in such high-handed, ham-fisted and totally arrogant behaviour — rendering quite counter-productive the state visit for which he himself had pushed.

Fidel's Follies

Although I served, over the years, at widely separated Canadian embassies in Latin America — in Mexico, Uruguay and Colombia with accreditation also to Ecuador — my work rarely brought proximity with that most restless of Latin American travellers, Cuba's peripatetic prime minister, Fidel Castro.

In fact the closest contact I ever had, however slight, was one day at United Nations headquarters in New York when — complete with fatigues, cigar and henchmen — he plopped down beside me in the delegates' lounge and we exchanged a few pleasantries in Spanish.

It took a couple of more years — till December 1971 — before I got another, and quite astonishing, look at the Cuban leader, even though we were separated by the two hundred miles that lie between Guayaquil, the large port-city of Ecuador, and Quito, its capital, 9,200 feet up in the Andes. The gap between us was intimately bridged through the medium of close-up tv videotape.

Since, at that time, Ecuador did not have diplomatic relations with Cuba, how did Castro manage to get himself invited to Guayaquil, of all unlikely places, and be received by the president of Ecuador and key members of his cabinet?

Castro's travels within Latin America had for some years
been circumscribed by the quarantine imposed, on U.S.
initiative, by the Organization of American States, all but one
of whose members had severed relations with Cuba. This
made him *persona non grata* throughout the hemisphere.

It was in 1971, after Chile became the first Western nation
to vote an avowed Marxist — Salvador Allende — into
power, that Castro felt able to break out of the OAS leash. He
contrived to be invited for an official ten-day visit to Chile,
where President Allende received him with acclaim. The
main thing that went wrong on that occasion was that, to the
discomfiture of his hosts, Castro just stayed on — and on,
and managed to extend his visit to over three weeks — a
"marathon," the Chileans called it.

Before returning to Havana, Castro arranged another key
breakthrough — a brief visit to Lima, to meet with the
highly nationalistic and non-Marxist but collectivist-minded
military leaders who were then governing Peru.

Even more surprising was the suddenly announced "technical stopover" he would be making in Guayaquil on his way
back to Cuba. This visit, however, required no contriving by
Castro. Although purportedly necessary to service his plane,
the stopover was, in fact, contrived by the president of
Ecuador, abetted by two of his key ministers.

Ecuador's president at the time was the Grand Old Man of
Ecuadorian politics — the five-times elected and four-times
deposed José Maria Velasco Ibarra. At seventy-eight years of
age, he was a tall, erect, patriarchal figure, of austere and
dignified bearing, who expected those about him —
certainly a visiting head of government, no matter of what
political hue — to comport themselves similarly. Furthermore, his chief of protocol had recently returned from
Stockholm and, with the president's blessing, seemed determined to inflict the stiff protocol of the Swedish Royal Court
on the officialdom of this turbulent mountainous Andean
republic.

President Velasco had called for new elections, and his

main motive in manoeuvering Castro's "technical stopover" was to gain support, or at least to forestall opposition, from growingly restive student groups and from the workers of Guayaquil. Furthermore, the president prided himself on being a historian, and he may not have been able to resist the temptation to meet a genuinely historical personality of modern Latin America — indeed of the world — and thus, inferentially, enhance his own historical image.

Although Ecuador's Armed Forces abhorred the idea of the visit — they refused to mount a military ceremony in Castro's honour — the minister of national defence was all for it; it might serve to achieve extradition of the young Ecuadorians who had hijacked a plane to Cuba. The newly appointed minister of foreign affairs — an admirer of the regime in Peru — was all for it; if Castro was going to visit Lima, he should also visit Guayaquil, if not Quito, notwithstanding the absence of diplomatic relations.

None of the foreign diplomats in Quito were invited to Guayaquil, not even the Soviet ambassador, although he had gone down on instructions to organize flight clearance and fuel for Castro's expected Ilyushin. That plane never arrived because the Peruvians had lent Fidel a plane of their own to get him back to Havana.

These were the antecedents of the *opéra-bouffe* that Castro was to stage, to the astonishment of his hosts, in the sweltering heat of Ecuador's equatorial port city.

Imagine the austere and correctly garbed Ecuadorian president's surprise: when Fidel Castro emerged from his plane in fatigues and sweaty shirt, with collar open down to his navel; when he stooped down to wipe off his heavy, dusty boots with his *right* hand — the one he proffered to his startled host; when Castro slapped him on the back and gave him a bear-like *abrazo*; and when he found himself immediately addressed by Castro with the familiar *tu*.

When the party moved inside, everyone disengaged to allow the president and his Cuban guest to hold a private conversation. Re-establishment of diplomatic relations? The tuna-boat war with the United States? Ecuador's new discoveries of oil? North-South, East-West? We shall never know, because the tv sound equipment was turned off. But someone forgot to screen the pair with curtains. In full view of the delighted press and the television cameramen, Castro repeatedly slapped his seventy-eight-year-old host on the back, and President Velasco attempted to sidle away with each slap — like a reluctant damsel being courted by a vagabond.

When the official luncheon got under way, Castro, with his chair tilted back and his stretched-out legs spread wide, ate his shrimps and lobster with his fingers, asking the president how — since the food in Ecuador was so good — he could stay as thin as a skeleton. Throughout the meal Fidel banged his glass with his fork to interrupt other guests' conversations. He leapt up and down at the table and, often with mouth full, shouted from one end to the other. Towards the end of the meal he asked for more champagne which — possibly because of the improvised circumstances of the arrangements in Guayaquil — had by that time run out. So he leaned over the guest next to him and, with a boarding-house reach, seized the still-full glass of the startled foreign minister of Ecuador. As one local newspaper put it the next day, Castro left one of the prime architects of his breakthrough visit to Ecuador without either a drink or a foreign policy.

During the speech-making, Castro told the minister of natural resources — responsible for Ecuador's newly found petroleum wealth — that he "stank of oil." He referred to the Organization of American States as a "sewer" — possibly forgetting (or did he?) that then OAS Secretary-General Galo Plaza was one of the most revered of living Ecuadorians and that Ecuador was a staunch supporter of the inter-American body.

For his part, President Velasco attempted to display a little political pluralism. Ecuadorians, he said, might not share Castro's political views but they did admire his achievements in Cuba and admire him as a person; and they realized that he suffered the pains and tribulations of Cuba on his very flesh. With less than gallantry, Castro replied by asking why, if the president so approved the Cuban revolution and himself, he did not carry out a similar revolution in Ecuador, "which it was in his power to do."

And so it went.

While Fidel Castro clearly enjoyed twitting the tails of his hosts, about the only ones in Ecuador to derive anything from his visit were the press, who not only enjoyed a field day but found the courage to indulge in criticism of the authorities to a degree that they had not dared express hitherto. As one Quito daily put it, the president of the republic and five senior ministers went to meet a mere prime minister of a country with which they had no relations, at an airport far from the capital, during a technical stop for a plane that required no servicing. "Fraud" and "fiasco" was the media consensus.

Cuba-watchers subsequently informed me that this *enfant terrible* act of Castro's in Guayaquil was "par for the course," although they also assured me that the Cuban prime minister, *when* he wished, could behave as properly as any head of government in the hemisphere.

And as for President Velasco Ibarra, I could not help but feel sad at the thought of such humiliation in the twilight of an extraordinary political career. I was one of the few foreign diplomats who knew that — not for any political or personal gain but out of a sense of abiding humanity — he had been quietly responsible for enabling some of the human flotsam and jetsam who survived World War II death camps to begin new lives, in Andean-Indian Ecuador.

The Difference Between...

In autumn, my thoughts often go back more than a quarter century to an odd little episode that took place just after I arrived in Mexico City to take up the post of first secretary at the Canadian Embassy. In retrospect, it turned out to be unique in my three-decade Canadian foreign service career.

In 1955 I had been working as United States desk officer in the Department of External Affairs in Ottawa. When I was offered the post in Mexico, and after talking it over with Crenia, I eagerly accepted and began studying Spanish for the first time. In addition, I began reading about Mexico. For the most part, that country's history and international relations seemed to be inextricably intertwined with her huge neighbour to the North.

As I read on, I soon became appalled to read about Mexico's tortuous relations with the United States, exacerbated by the American conquest over the years of such prime real estate as California, Texas, Arizona and New Mexico. But even more appalling was what I read about the behaviour of American petroleum and mining corporations and their buccaneering personnel in Mexico. I was reading American, not Mexican, histories, and they conveyed a caricature of the worst features of nineteenth-century big-stick imperialism.

Mexico is quintessentially a *mestizo* (mixed race) country; the bulk of its population combines Aztec, other Indian, and Spanish bloods, with negro admixtures in certain areas. There is a small minority of whites. Prejudice about race and colour seem all the more intolerable in the Mexican *mestizo* setting. Mexican hypersensitivities to, and resentment of, everything American pervaded the works that I read. And they seemed hardly less pervasive when my family and I arrived in Mexico City in September of 1955.

The American Embassy in Mexico is one of the United States' largest, and I assumed that its staff would have been selected for their understanding of, and sensitivity to, Mexican complexes about colour and race and to Mexico's manifold concerns about relations with its then dominant neighbour. Indeed, on perusing the American Embassy's personnel list in the local diplomatic handbook, I noted that the labour attaché was Ben Stephansky; I had read that the Mexican authorities esteemed him greatly for his sensitive handling of the complex *bracero* (wetback) illegal immigration problem, as divisive then as it is now. The revered ex-president, Lazaro Cardenas, had said that Ben had a better understanding of the problem and its impact on Mexican-United States relations than anyone in Mexico.

And I was delighted to see in the diplomatic list that my opposite number in the U.S. Embassy was Bill Snow. Bill had been Canadian desk officer in the State Department while I was U.S. desk officer in Ottawa and, although we had never met, we knew of each other by remote control. External would get telegrams in Ottawa from our embassy in Washington saying, "Snow on the Canadian desk told us today that..." and the State Department undoubtedly received telegrams from its embassy in Ottawa referring occasionally to me as the source of some information.

Very quickly after arrival in Mexico City, I arranged to have a chat with Hugh Morgan, Number Two at the British

Embassy, and I fixed an appointment with Bill Snow for early the next afternoon.

Snow couldn't have been more friendly and helpful when I called on him. He gave me a run-down for nearly two hours on the important subjects and personalities of the day, and he then took me around his embassy to meet section chiefs who, he promised, would give me any help I might wish after settling in.

It was getting to be around four o'clock and I indicated, after profuse thanks for his helpfulness, that it was time for me to break away. But Bill insisted that I take a few more moments to meet his ambassador; he was, Bill had said, a political appointee of President Eisenhower's and, by profession, a Maryland banker.

Bill took me into the ambassador's office and introduced me. The ambassador opened the conversation by asking the usual question of a newcomer: where had I served prior to coming to Mexico. When I replied that I had just arrived from Ottawa, where I had been serving on the United States desk, he asked whether I had ever served at the Canadian Embassy in Washington.

To this I replied that, regrettably, I had never served in Washington and hardly knew the city at all. But, I went on to say, I had worked for many years in New York before joining External Affairs and then at our Consulate General and Permanent Mission to the United Nations.

"Oh you must know New York well, then," said the ambassador. "Do you know what we in Maryland say is the difference between Washington and New York?"

Sensing that I should play the "straight man" for a joke, I said: "No, Mr Ambassador, what do people in Maryland say is the difference between Washington and New York?"

"Well," the ambassador replied, "Up in Maryland we say that in Washington you get pushed around by the niggers and in New York you get pushed around by the Jews."

I shall never forget the look on Bill Snow's face as he blanched and froze. In a grim voice, hardly audible, he told the ambassador that he had already taken too much of his time and that he knew I had to go on to another appointment. We quickly left the room.

Nearly speechless on our way to the elevators, I thanked Bill for the useful briefing he had given me and how interesting it was that — after being opposite numbers for many months in Ottawa and Washington — we had finally met up in Mexico City.

But I thought it the path of wisdom *not* to mention to Bill that I indeed was in a hurry to get to my next appointment — to meet my family for dinner before sundown and then go on, for the first time in Mexico, to take part in the Kol Nidre services, which begin Yom Kippur, the Day of Atonement.

Uruguay, Briefly

Towards the end of a tour of duty at our Permanent Mission to the United Nations, I was appointed resident chargé d'affaires of the Canadian Embassy in Uruguay. Crenia and I arrived in Montevideo at the end of August 1969, happy with the prospects of our new, although modest, post.

About six weeks after we arrrived in Montevideo, the Canadian Thanksgiving holiday had come around and we spent the day at our new home-away-from-home, hanging the last of the paintings we had brought with us; I had finished calls at the foreign ministry and on diplomatic colleagues; and we had met the handful of local Canadian residents. Our Spanish abilities were returning after an eleven-year hiatus.

Late on Thanksgiving morning the telephone rang. A Canadian clerk had passed by the office on the holiday and found the telex machine clattering long messages in cipher. He had deciphered a few lines. He urged me to come down immediately to the chancery.

Two confidential telegrams had arrived from Ottawa — one from Mitchell Sharp, secretary of state for external affairs, the other from Under-Secretary Marcel Cadieux.

What they added up to was simple — and jolting: for reasons of austerity, the government was reducing the number of persons of all ranks stationed abroad and, as part of this process, was closing down eight posts entirely, three of them in Latin America and one of which was Montevideo. I was instructed to seek an urgent appointment with the Uruguayan foreign minister to inform him that we would be closing out the embassy within four months. Our Uruguayan employees were to be given notice, the Department would attempt to arrange cross-postings for our Canadian staff, and I was to return to Ottawa for re-assignment. Leases were to be cancelled, contracts annulled, and furniture, vehicles and other items were to be disposed of or shipped to other posts, as would be subsequently directed by the Department.

So began the final four months of our short stay in Montevideo, during which I had to terminate our fine, loyal and shocked Uruguayan employees, negotiate transfers of our Canadian staff and totally liquidate our small diplomatic mission,. My first task that morning was to seek an urgent appointment with Foreign Minister Venancio Flores and tell him this astounding news.

In October 1969, Uruguay was a tense nation. A strike of banking employees was paralyzing the country. The old-line Colorado and Blanco parties were at loggerheads, and Congress seemed paralyzed. Tupamaro urban guerrilla tactics were becoming bolder — they had just staged a spectacular rescue of imprisoned comrades by digging an escape tunnel out of Montevideo's main prison. To bolster exports there was a ban on the domestic sale of beef — the three-meals-a-day staple of every Uruguayan's diet.

For Canada — of all admired countries — to close its embassy and scuttle out of the country would be ominous and foreboding. With these thoughts in mind, I went downtown to keep my appointment.

I explained to Mr Venancio Flores that because of economic conditions in Canada, our government had decided to reduce its diplomatic and consular staff around the world and that, as part of this process, it was closing eight of its diplomatic missions — of which Montevideo was to be one.

The foreign minister looked at me in shocked astonishment, then, in a sad voice, he replied. "Mr chargé d'affaires, I imagine that to be instructed to come here and to tell me this must be difficult and painful for you, especially after having arrived so recently. I will say simply this. Please tell your government that Uruguay, too, knows what it is to experience economic difficulties and to have to introduce measures of austerity. We, too, have had to close several of our missions abroad in recent years. But, just as we found that we could manage subsequently to re-open our missions, we are confident that Canada, too, will find that it is able to do the same thing." He then went on to assure me of his ministry's co-operation to facilitate our closing-down procedures and to liquidate or transfer our contracts and property. Fortunately, he had not learned that, on that same day, Ottawa was announcing the opening of new posts at the Vatican and in Africa.

Although it was not customary for the foreign ministry to fete departing heads of mission, my hosts not only did so but held their luncheon for me in the penthouse dining room of Montevideo's leading hotel, co-hosted by the under-secretary of foreign affairs and the director-general of the ministry. It was attended by the directors-general of all branches and their heads of division. Word must have gone out that this was a must; the ministry was on a summer timetable and many of these officers had already moved down the coast to Punta del Este.

The director-general of the ministry, Sr Marques Sere, whom I had known when he was Uruguay's permanent representative at the United Nations, opened the farewell remarks. He took the line that there was no other country in the world for which Uruguay had greater respect; that Uruguayans were a genuinely democratic people and Canadians occupied a special place in their hearts; that Canada had achieved a special place in the western world and had played an extraordinary role in multilateral organizations; that the reputation of our foreign service was second to none; that living herself alongside giant and powerful neighbours, Uruguay had a special interest in Canadian policies; that Uruguay had been going through trying times and needed the support of her friends, amongst whom she counted Canada foremost during this difficult period; and that it would be difficult to conceive of Montevideo without a resident Canadian mission and, after our present difficulties were over, we would surely find it possible to return. This line, au revoir but not farewell — was echoed by other officers through the luncheon.

It was a hard act to follow. I emphasized that our decision to close had been dictated by harsh budgetary considerations only, and should not be construed in any way as reflecting any diminution of our appreciation of the unique place that Uruguay occupied in South America, or of her superb performance on the international stage and in multilateral organizations, such as the United Nations, where we had co-operated closely. I emphasized that nothing would change in our relationship with Uruguay except the modalities of conducting our local business; our ambassador in Buenos Aires and other officers at our embassy there were accredited to Uruguay and would henceforth make frequent visits to ensure that the happy and close relationship between our two countries would continue unchanged.

A week later, at the end of January 1970, and barely six months after arriving, Crenia and I were on a plane for the long flight back to Rio, New York and re-assignment in February's Ottawa.

Hither
and Yon

Diplomatic Verse:
The Poets of External

External Affairs' early files contain surprising treasures. One epic example was inspired by the government's post-World War II decree forbidding External's personnel from accepting foreign decorations "either for war service or otherwise, except for distinguished services in the saving of life."

Under the wartime and early postwar leadership of a great under-secretarial team, Norman Robertson and Hume Wrong, and, at a lower level, of Lester B. Pearson and Hugh Keenleyside, most External personnel had, in fact, made great personal sacrifices during the war.

And, at a more junior level, there was Alfred Rive. He had been severely wounded during World War I, in which he lost one eye, and he had toiled tirelessly for External throughout World War II, dealing with prisoner-of-war and Canadian internee problems. After World War II, he was given his first head-of-post assignment as — by his own admission — the Not-So-Very High Commissioner to New Zealand. When he received notification, while in Wellington, of the government's ukase forbidding acceptance by External personnel of foreign decorations, he was inspired to write a touching lament, in verse, which he sent off to Under-Secretary Mike

Pearson. I served under Alfred Rive for three years at the
Canadian Embassy in Dublin, and never did I know a kinder
or more gentle soul in External. But I was unaware of his
talent for poetry nor, for that matter, did I then suspect the
sense of humour that inspired the verses that had been sent
by him to Mr Pearson.

Attention: L.B. Pearson, Esq., O.B.E. November 25th, 1946

> Sir, I have the honour to
>   Acknowledge your dictations,
> In your despatch two fifty-six,
>   Concerning decorations.
>
> When first I was an F.S.O.
>   "third Sec." the designation's,
> I thought "Some day my chest will show
>   Some simple decorations."
>
> As "Second Sec." I carried on,
>   More work and more vexations,
> Sustained by thoughts that to be won
>   Were various decorations.
>
> The years went by, I was a "First."
>   I had no more vacations.
> My high ambition still I nursed —
>   Some rows of decorations.
>
> As Counsellor I counselled well
>   And hid my palpitations.
> "How near" I thought, "no one can tell —
>   Those glamorous decorations."
>
> And so, as slow I struggled through
>   External's permutations,
> I saw myself in distant view
>   Bedecked with decorations.

Through thick and thin, as near or far
　　Were my perambulations,
I hitched my wagon to a star
　　And other decorations.

But as I neared the goal apace,
　　And told all my relations,
External sent a blunt ukase
　　"You'll get no decorations.

"We'll put you in no Honours List
　　With flattering citations.
We think your name will not be missed
　　No stars — no decorations!

"Nor will it help you to ally
　　With foreign delegations.
The rigid rule will still apply
　　No stars — no decorations!"

　　　　I have the honour, Sir, to be
　　　　　　(Quite without berations)
　　　　C.M., C.B., O.B.E.,
　　　　　　(Or other decorations).

　　　　Your very humble (Sir, that's me)
　　　　　　Accept felicitations,
　　　　Obedient servant, (you'll agree)
　　　　　　Bereft of decorations.

　　　　(Sgd.) Alfred Rive
　　　　Not Very High Commissioner

Now Mr Pearson's sense of humour had, by 1947, become
legendary in External's circles, and given the occasion that
Mr Rive's poem afforded, he fired off the following reply.

Ottawa, 5th February, 1947

Dear Alfred:

I am deeply moved by your poetic lament in your unnumbered despatch of November 25th, in which you revealed your bitter disappointment at being deprived of decorations.

I wracked my brains trying to compose a suitable reply but with no success, so at Hume's suggestion I called upon the poetic talent of the East Block, with the offer of a bottle of whiskey as a bait for the best poetic rejoinder to your tale of frustrated ambition.

The results were most successful and as all the entries were of such excellence, I have decided to send you the lot. The prize was awarded to Stuart Hemsley for the first poem in the attached collection, but it was difficult to choose and you may prefer one of the others. The authors initials are given in each case. I should perhaps warn you that this whole collection, together with your original poem, has been circulated to all our missions, so you may well be assailed with verse from all corners of the globe. I am not sure whether this action will put an end to versification by heads of missions or whether it will start a flood of poetry which we will be unable to stop...

Yours sincerely,
L. B. Pearson

Surprisingly, the Department, and Alfred Rive in far-off Wellington, were deluged with rhyme — although, even more surprisingly, nothing was received from External's most distinguished poets, Robert Ford and Douglas LePan. What follows is the Bottle-of-Scotch prize-winning verse-in-reply, which came from Stuart Hemsley, who, at that time, was serving in External at headquarters.

Ottawa, January 18, 1947
Reply to Alfred Rive, Esq., O.S.C.

Sir,

With a sense of deep emotion
    I approach your rhymed lament;
For I never had a notion
    That you crave embellishment,
Longed to make a clanging entry
With be-medalled foreign gentry.

Though a rose, you blushed unheeded,
    Fruitless always was your quest
Of the medal sorely needed
    For your Diplomatic chest.
Not a ribbon on his sternum!
Though he strive, he may not earn 'em.

May not? Hold! 'tis when they're broken
    By exception rules are prove-
'd. Let's design some little token;
    Let's get Alfred in the groove!
Beat the cymbal, sound the clarion!
Pin a medal where there's nary 'un!

Something neat — not like the whopper
    That your foreign envoy wears;
But more suited to the proper
    Corps of High Commissionaires.
Something for our dignitaori,
On his mission to the Maori.

So I cooked a neat Submission,
    Cooked it, Alfred, just for you;
Rectifying past omission,
    'Twas the least that I could do.
Mov'd by Council's Topmost Genie!
Passed, and signed by Arnold Heeney!

Thus by awful dispensation,
Compensating years of loss,
Fitting is your decoration;-
Order of the Southern Cross.
Take your Cross and either wear it,
Or, in silence, grin and bear it.

Stuart Hemsley

Mr Pearson then concluded this episode in the poetic life of External Affairs by sending the following letter to Hume Wrong, who was by then Canada's ambassador in Washington:

Ottawa, 5th February 1947

Dear Hume:

Your suggestion in your letter of January 3rd that a bottle of whiskey should be offered for the best reply in verse to Alfred Rive's poetic lament has revealed a wealth of poetic talent in the East Block.

The results have been so cheering that I decided to circulate the whole collection in the attached sheets. The prize was awarded to Mr Hemsley, but only after much critical consideration. The other competitors were compensated however, as Stuart held a party in Ronnie Macdonnell's office and the honours were shared by all the poets.

Sidney Pierce took exception to your remark that he might show "unexpected gifts" and sent me the following message on receiving notice of the competition:

"Please advise the under-secretary that I shall compete in the competition and please convey to him the following:

Hume Wrong, our representative
To Uncle Sam's great nation,
Suspects my 'unexpected Gift'
At rhythmical creation.

I urge that L.B. (Mike) have this
In officers implanted:-
'Your *own* gifts you may unexpect
But others' take for granted.' "

Yours sincerely,
L.B. Pearson

Wife of...

Sondra Gotlieb, "wife of" Canada's ex-ambassador to the United States, has written wittily about the ignominious fate of some Washington wives, who, however talented in their own right, become known simply as appendages of their illustrious husbands — "wife of" the senator from, the ambassador to, the secretary of, or just the supreme court justice.

But, in Canada's foreign service, the shoe is sometimes on the other foot.

Out in the Philippines, for example, Ben Pflanz arrived with his family in 1981 happy with his appointment as counsellor at the Canadian Embassy in Manila. In short order, he became known simply as "husband of" Connie, the fleetest woman in the Philippines.

Just before the Philippines First International Marathon was to be held in Manila, the foreign office asked embassy people to do a short run to publicize the great event. Connie Pflanz, a mother of four from Calgary and in her forties, turned out and caught the bug. During her stay in Manila, she placed first for women in the Third World Marathon at 3:16:30 and, only two weeks later, she ran the Philippines International Marathon with an even better 3:10:36. She won, or was near the front, in dozens of other ten-to-twenty-kilometre events during her stay, all of them run in un-Canadian mid-nineties temperatures. As a housewife back home in Calgary, Connie's physical fitness consisted mainly in shovelling snow, cutting the grass, tending the garden and walking to the grocery store. Connie must surely be the only External spouse who, if attending a reception after a marathon, had a painful struggle to put high-heeled shoes on swollen runner's feet.

All this put Connie constantly on national tv and radio and on the front pages of the newspapers, and she became a national figure not only for winning marathons: she single-handedly popularized running amongst Philippine women.

And Ben? He became simply "husband of" the champ. It took an official visit by Prime Minister Trudeau to get him invited to the Marcos' Palace, although Connie had been there as a guest, twice. When the Pflanz family departed the Philippines, Ben noticed that the newspapers read by fellow-passengers in their plane all front-paged fond farewells — to Connie.

This scene now shifts to the other side of the world, to Norway, where Ed Skrabec arrived in 1981 to serve as counsellor of the Canadian Embassy in Oslo, with his wife, Iris. For their first Christmas Eve, they invited 125 diplomatic and local Canadian guests for a buffet dinner.

For this affair Iris, from Gimli, Manitoba, planned for a main dish to serve two fifteen-pound salmon. And how does a Manitoba housewife manage to prepare these in a modest kitchen, every facility of which would be already strained to turn out hams, turkeys, trimmings, cakes and pies?

Back in Gimli, all Iris ever knew about salmon was to empty it out of a tin. But the ambassador's wife, Mrs Kenneth Wardroper, had passed on a tip — don't boil a salmon, steam it. And the best way to do that is to wrap it in foil, place it in the electric dishwasher and just turn the washer on, not just for one cycle but for three or four. Iris's dishwasher-steamed

whole salmon was the talk of the party, and by Christmas
Day had become the talk of Oslo.

Now, in Norway, salmon figures large in the national
consciousness, like beef in Argentina and snails and truffles
in France. Any gimmick to improve the preparing or con-
serving of salmon takes on national importance.

Iris was asked to dishwasher-steam salmon on national
television and for newspaper and magazine writers. She

found herself greeted by complete strangers in buses and
supermarkets. By New Year's Day, Iris and her dishwasher
salmon had become famous throughout Norway, and in the
great salmony Scandinavian Beyond.

After that Christmas Eve dinner, and with his nose to the
embassy grindstone, Ed Skrabec became just one more
Canadian "husband of."

Around the Parliamentary Press Gallery in Ottawa, Sean
Brady was well known as Joe Clark's spokesman. But while

serving at the Canadian Embassy in Bangkok, where he married a Thai beauty, he found he was just "husband of" Thailand's leading lady of the stage, Patravadee Sritriratana, known across the nation as Lek — not only an outstanding actress but also playwright, stage and film director, singer and dancer.

If these trends continue, men in the Canadian foreign service may soon have to push for some kind of affirmative action program. Any way you look at it, Sondra Gotlieb's creation, the ignominious "wife of" the masculine movers and shakers of this world, may yet end up as one more endangered species.

An In-House
(Out-House?) Tale

Readers of these tales will have realized by now that diplomacy isn't always accompanied by world-shaking events, and that Canada's foreign service officers must be prepared to cope with all kinds of situations and with all kinds of people. Diplomats should not only show versatility and virtuosity but possess — as the occasion may require — a sense of humour.

To illustrate, I will draw on an episode in the career of one of my favourite former colleagues, George Ignatieff. I had the good fortune to serve under George for two tours of duty — both at the United Nations. The first was in the late '40s, when George was principal adviser to General A.G.L. McNaughton, Canada's first ambassador and permanent representative to the United Nations. The second was in the late '60s, when George himself occupied that exalted position. Regretfully, I did not serve with him when he was Canadian ambassador to Yugoslavia for three years in between those stints at the UN. In taking up that post in Belgrade, he became the first foreign-born Canadian to be appointed a Canadian ambassador.

I know of nothing in our foreign service folklore to equal what befell Ignatieff one day in Belgrade. He refers to this episode in his memoirs, but he gave a much livelier account when he took part in a series of radio programs devoted to international affairs. I can't resist a wholesale borrowing from the CBC transcript of George Ignatieff's verbatim account of this venture into high diplomacy.

GI: One day a Mr Warwick came in from Blenheim, Ontario. He says, Are you one of the goddamn fools from External Affairs who doesn't know a pig from a sow? And I said, I am sorry, Mr Warwick, what has got you in this condition? Well, he said, I am a raiser of animals for sale. I have cattle and pigs and I raise hybrid corn. And, he said, I arrived in London the other day by air from Ontario. I had some semen, he said. People from External Affairs don't seem to know that you can't bring cattle across for sale. You bring specimens, for artificial insemination. He said, I had these things and the customs were creating difficulties, and I said I wanted to phone Canada House. The Canada House operator answers and says and what may I do for you? He said, look here, I am Mr Warwick from Blenheim, Ontario. I have got some semen for Romania here. And she said, oh, just one minute, I will connect you with the naval attaché. Mr Warwick was as mad as the dickens. He said that's the kind of ignorance, he said. Now what are you going to do to help? And I said, what do you want me to do? Well, he said, I have come here to make a sale of hybrid corn and some Landrace pigs, and I want you to help. I said fine. We went to see the minister of agriculture, and I made a sales pitch. I had to, since he couldn't speak any Serbo-Croatian. I had to translate part of it and support his pitch about corn. We got this sale through. Then Mr Warwick said, it comes to the Landrace pigs. Well, the minister said, now look, I have given you all the time I have; I really haven't any more time. Oh, Warwick said, now I have just got to talk to you about Landrace pigs. So then I said, I will do this in ten minutes you see. I said, look I

will get up and do the talking while you…and he said,
that's fine, you demonstrate the pig. And he got up and
he said, look, I am fat and paunchy. I've got big hams, he
says. From a protein point of view, I am not much of a
pig. Then he said, now look at the ambassador (and in
those days I was much leaner). He slapped my thighs and
my back and, he said, now, look, that's a good straight
side of bacon and that makes a good ham. Now, he said,
that is what I am trying to get across to you. If you buy

that product you are going to have good hams and
you're going to have good bacon, he said. Now that's
Landrace pigs. Now I promise to deliver you just a thing
like this. And there I was modelling a pig. Now, I never
expected to do that in diplomacy, but that's what you get
down to in the rough-and-tumble of representing your
country's interests. You have got to be willing to turn
your hand to anything.

A versatile foreign officer indeed!

Alarms
from Ankara

While the majority of Canada's ambassadors and high commissioners are appointed from career foreign service personnel, the government occasionally instructs External to appoint someone from outside. The government does this for a variety of reasons — sometimes as a reward for some political debt or to lessen some awkward individual's proximity to the seat of power.

But outstanding non-career appointees have included such stalwarts as George Drew, Paul Martin, and General A.G.L. McNaughton.

And then there was General Victor Odlum, one of the most colourful characters ever to serve as a Canadian ambassador. Prime Minister King originally appointed him, in 1940, as Canada's first high commissioner to Australia. This was done, to put it frankly, in order to relieve the prime minister of a political embarrassment — of having him command the Second Canadian Division. Once ensconced in Canberra, General Odlum strove with much vigour to have Canadian forces engage in Pacific defence; so much so that this caused certain problems to arise with the Australian government, and Mr King decided that it was the path of wisdom to appoint Odlum as ambassador to China when we opened a post in Nanking in 1943. Well, once a general, always a general: Odlum ran his post in Nanking with his accustomed military élan, somewhat to the consternation of his colleagues in the embassy. Some resented being ordered around and inspected at any hour as if on parade, and for no apparent reason other than to satisfy the General's wishes to be a commanding officer.

General Odlum's next appointment, in 1948, was as Canadian ambassador to Turkey. In Ankara, he quickly found another quite surprising avenue in which he could indulge his military flare.

In the spring of 1948, with the Cold War mounting, there was some concern that the Soviet Union might one day invade Western Europe, and if it did so, that it would invade through Greece and Turkey. In this eventuality the General, assuming that his likely European route of evacuation from Ankara would be cut off by the prior invasion of Greece, informed the Department in Ottawa (which was quite relaxed on the subject and had given Odlum no instructions in the matter) that he had devised his own plan of escape. In a TOP SECRET despatch to Ottawa he wrote:

As I have not heard from you, I must assume that you have not been able to picture a probable situation and, as a consequence, have neither directions nor advice to give at the present moment. I am not at all surprised at this, for it must be more difficult for you than it is for me to envisage what is likely to happen.

I have, naturally, because it is my custom to do so, made plans of my own. To these I will adhere unless, before it is necessary to put them into effect, I receive other instructions from you. They are based upon the prime consideration that the only transport facilities we will have under our own control will be our motorcars. At the present moment, we have three of these. I am informed that Colonel Bingham's car has already left New York. I would make immediate use of at least three of these cars and with

them send (possibly) Colonel Bingham and (certainly) Mr
Cox with the majority of the members of the staff. They
would travel by overland route heading for Beirut, in
Syria. I would remain behind myself and might keep
Colonel Bingham with me. I would not feel like leaving
Ankara until it had been agreed by the Turkish govern-
ment, as well as by my senior colleagues in the diplomatic
corps, that a move was necessary.

It is true that here in Ankara, we have not as many
administrative problems requiring last minute attention as
rest on the shoulders of the Canadian ambassador in
Athens. There are a good many Canadians in Greece; but
there are few, if any, Canadians in Turkey for whom we
would have to assume responsibility. The number is certainly negligible. In any event, we could not do much for
them because those who are here in Turkey are out of our
reach. We have no facilities which we could place at their
disposal in any event. My major task would be to look
after the embassy staff and records, and to keep you
advised up to the last moment.

In order to be able to carry out the program I have in
mind, it would be necessary to secure, at some early stage, a
number of drums of petrol and with them a supply of oil.
We would keep these stored and ready for emergency. We
ought to have one vehicle which could play the part of a
truck to carry our heavier material as well as the supply of
petrol. It is true that there are petrol stations between here
and Beirut; but, under the circumstances which would
certainly prevail, we could not be sure that their supplies of
petrol would be available for us. The petrol in the tanks
would probably be requisitioned by military authorities.

If you concur in my major suggestion, I think it would
be wise to have a sturdy truck shipped to Ankara. This
truck would be most valuable in any event. It would be
invaluable in case of evacuation.

There are financial aspects to the situation concerning
which I have already written you. I have asked that an

emergency fund be placed at my disposal in the form of physical currency, to be held in a reserve until the worst comes or, in the alternative, until the whole situation clears up.

As long as signal communications continue, I would be able to keep in touch with you and to get last min-ute instructions. At the same time I know that, as General LaFlèche (Canadian ambassador in Athens) has suggested, communication systems may become badly disorganized. Even if not disorganized, they will certainly be so con-gested that I could not be sure that messages would get through.

I am sure that, through my Arab friends, I would be given all necessary protection and assistance in travelling through Syria, Lebanon, Iraq, Arabia and *parts* of Pal-estine. Moreover, through them and in Egypt, I would be able to secure local funds in any grave emergency.

At an early date a substantial shipment of canned goods and supplies, ordered last fall, will arrive from Eaton's in Toronto. An ample reserve will be set aside for use *only* if and when it may be necessary to move out of Turkey under pressure.

Fortunately, and perhaps with some foresight, I brought with me camping equipment, including knives, forks, plates, cups and cooking utensils. Moreover, there are two camp beds and with them, a 'roll' table and folding canvas chairs. These would provide comfortable travelling accommodation for my wife and Mrs Cox. The rest would have to adjust themselves to 'service' condi-tions and customs. As a matter of fact, even without any help from you, I am reasonably prepared to face any emergency; but a truck, primarily to carry a supply of petrol, would certainly be of great assistance. It is true that my camping kit was not designed for so many people; but by second and even third 'sittings', it could be made to do. I even have a South African canvas water bag, and a small Australian silk tent!

On receipt of this (unique) despatch in Ottawa, External sent the General neither additional funds for the purchase of petrol, nor did it send him a truck. A year later he was again writing to the under-secretary to update his evacuation plans in case of a USSR attack by an air strike. Not to be defeated by the Department's unhelpful reluctance to get off its hind quarters, the General had devised his own means of acquiring a truck in the event of the anticipated emergency.

Assuming that from the first hour communication would be gone and that all traffic, including air, would be in confusion, I turned my thoughts to transport by motorcar and truck. These could be under our own control. Reference to previous despatches on this subject will show that I have not changed my mind. In fact, my opinions are held more firmly than ever.

I admit that there is a school of thought which believes that Turkey, being tough, will not be attacked, but will, instead, be side-tracked. The many who think this way are taking the situation very light-heartedly and are making no preparations.

For my own part, I cannot adhere to this school. It would be very wrong for me to do so, unless I had sound grounds for my convictions. Instead of having such grounds, my mind turns in an entirely different direction, as will be disclosed in the despatch referred to above; and so I feel it my duty to provide for the worst eventuality, not for the best.

To evacuate the last embassy group (after all records have been destroyed) by motorcar would mean:
(a) Sufficient cars *and* a truck, the latter to carry gasoline and supplies;
(b) Reserve gasoline (since the purchase of gasoline at that time would almost certainly be impossible);
(c) Reserve food supplies (for the same reason);
(d) *Usable currency* — Turkish lira, U.S. dollars or gold.

I have consistently assumed that a route to the north would be an impossible one; that the coastal harbours of Turkey would be in confusion (under bombs, as was Boulogne when I tried to get out of France in 1940); and that the only feasible route would be to the south, through the Arab countries.

Believing those things, I set out to make concrete plans. We have three passenger cars; and we *could* use the stationwagon as a truck, if necessary, but it would hardly be strong enough to carry a substantial load over the bad Turkish roads. A six-wheel truck would be much more reliable — and for one of these I have made arrangements. But I will only buy it in emergency. I have Turkish lira and U.S. dollars in the bank — although I have not yet suc-ceeded in changing the latter into physical currency. (This I expect to do before the summer is over.) I have put aside a reserve of gasoline — as the embassy accounts will show. I have adequate reserve food in storage and so I am nearly ready…

You will ask why I show so much concern at a time when a 'peace' propaganda is the major feature of the moment and while everywhere — except in China, Burma, Malaya, Indonesia and Greece — the air is so quiet that it is almost somnolent. Hitler's attack on Rus-sia was a 'noisy' one and its preparations were obvious to all observers. But the Russians do not think or act as Hitler did. With them everything is screened be-hind veils of distance and silence. If and when they strike, it will probably be just as silently and with great speed…

In a letter I received a few days ago from General Pope (head of the Canadian military mission in Berlin), he made reference to the fact that from every quarter come reports that there is neither tension nor apparent preparation for aggressive movement. General Pope very shrewdly added that when all men talk that way it is time for some men to be on their guard!

The saga of General Odlum in External's files does not end here, since he continued to bombard Ottawa with further despatches on other evacuation procedures that he was devising, such as how he used petty cash to purchase small quantities of sodium nitrate and sodium chlorate, which he had used to conduct experiments in the chemical destruction of documents, before requesting Ottawa to ship him (by *separate* diplomatic sea bags in order to avoid an explosion) sufficient quantities of these chemicals for the anticipated emergency. In view of how ill-prepared External Affairs had been to assist Canadian citizens who found themselves in the path of the German invasion of Western Europe in 1940, General Odlum's anxieties were not entirely without foundation; but, as usual, they were overdrawn.

Fortunately for both himself and the Department of External Affairs, the General's plans for evacuation from Turkey never had to be activated. The protracted telegraphic battle between a Department which sought to moderate or, more often, ignore his plans and his pleas for help in implementing them, and a military ambassador determined above all to carry them through was, happily, avoided by a more peaceful trend in world events, at least in the European theatre.

Angling My Way
Through External

In midsummer of 1951, Canada's Department of External Affairs became responsible for my becoming an avid flycaster. Three decades later, I was awarded a fly-casting world's record by the International Game Fish Association. (In serious angling circles, it's like winning Olympic gold.)

And how was External responsible? I began working at headquarters for the first time in 1951, after several years of New York and salt-water surfcasting (with conventional and spinning tackle) behind me. Feeling piscatorially lonely in Ottawa, I soon began going out to the Gatineau lakes area to fish for small-mouth bass — my first experience with fresh-water fishing — and I was using light spinning tackle. Rowing and casting by myself around Grand Lake one overcast June morning, rain suddenly began pouring down, drenching me to the skin.

I heard a voice in the distance between thunderbolts, and at a cottage on a small island in the centre of the lake, I spotted a man on the verandah waving me to come in out of the storm. After a cup of hot tea we were chatting; it came out that my host was retired from the old Department of Trade and Commerce, and that his daughter, Dorothy Morphy, worked in External for the assistant under-secretary across the hall from me.

Mr Morphy explained that he had had to give up fishing after suffering a heart attack, and had devoted himself to tying trout and salmon flies and bass bugs. He insisted on giving me a generous sample and urged me to give up spinning tackle and get on to the real sport — flycasting. I started using Mr Morphy's flies the next week, and I have never turned back. His gift included Parmachene Belles, Dark Montreals, Hendricksons, elk-hair dry caddis, Wooly Buggers — a gorgeous collection.

It's fortunate that, in retrospect, I was able to create some small impression of being a dedicated and hard-working member of the foreign service; otherwise, unkind critics might have insinuated that I joined External simply to expand my piscatorial horizons.

I had been an ardent angler long before entering External Affairs. Before the war, Crenia and I had moved from Manhattan to Long Island, and it was there that I became an enthusiastic surfcaster, pursuing the elusive striped bass all the way from Rockaway Inlet, in the shadows of Manhattan, along Long Island's south shore to Montauk Point, 120 miles out in the Atlantic.

Later, while serving at our Consulate General in New York and then at the United Nations, I managed to get in a few hours of surfcasting over most weekends, starting as early as the middle of February for flounders and carrying on into December if the mackerel were still running.

The top surfcasting season for Long Island unfortunately coincided with the annual General Assemblies of the United Nations which, under the Charter, frustratingly began in mid-September and dragged on towards Christmas. Whoever dreamed up that provision of the UN Charter couldn't have been a Long Island surfcaster.

Notwithstanding the UN's autumn turmoil, I usually managed to get in my early morning Saturday or Sunday surfcasting, but only with difficulty during 1948-49 and 1967-68, when Canada was a member of the Security Council and we were likely to be called for emergency meetings at any hour of the day or night. As if this did not make serious fishing difficult enough, certain workaholic zealots like George Ignatieff, when he was our permanent representative to the United Nations during our hectic years on the Security Council in 1967-68, had the unfortunate habit of calling delegation meetings for nine o'clock on a Saturday morning. These meetings did not present an insurmountable obstacle, however. My habit was to fish from five or six until eight in the morning and then return home. If a Saturday morning delegation meeting had been called, I would head straight for the office from the beach, sneak into a washroom to take off my chest waders and rain gear and, as the meeting droned on, wonder whether I smelled of bait and what fast action I was missing out on the Long Island shore.

Just as I was beginning to think that I was Externally alone in my obsession, I discovered that there were other — and, if possible, even worse — angling nuts within the austere precincts of the Department. My piscatorial co-enthusiasts included the ebullient Charles Eustache McGaughey — "McGuff" as he was universally known — who was considered a Far Eastern specialist but was really a denizen of the Ontario bush. His father had been a ranger in Algonquin Park, and McGuff used to spend his summer leave in an incredible shack way back in the bush, living on peanut-butter-and-onion sandwiches which, he explained when I went out one summer to fish Algonquin Park trout with him, were made from the only foodstuffs that kept well out there.

Another keen External fisherman was John Dougan, whose postings I used to eye nervously to see who was getting the fishiest move. I have never really forgiven him for getting the high commissionership to New Zealand, where he would have had fabulous trout fishing and big game fishing in salt water (if things hadn't changed since I read Zane Grey).

How widespread my piscatorial avidities were circulated

around External can be gauged by the greeting I got from
Chester Ronning in the spring of 1962 in New Delhi, where
he was serving as Canadian high commissioner, and where
my class at the National Defence College was visiting as part
of its Asian tour. When we arrived at New Delhi airport he
quickly took me aside to inform me that he had laid on a
short trout-fishing expedition for me in the Himalayas over a
weekend when my colleagues would be visiting the Taj
Mahal. He was very pleased with his foresight, and chagrined
when I told him — for some stupid and overzealous reason
— that I had better not break away from the group. To this
day I have been brooding over that decision.

If I missed out on New Zealand, I did receive one of the
finest piscatorial postings in our service — Ireland. Shortly
after arriving in Dublin in 1958, I became friendly with
George Burrows, the angling editor of that fine newspaper,
the *Irish Times*. George used to take me salmon fishing on a
beat (a length of shore) he had rented south of Dublin, on the
Slaney River. My neighbour in Simmonscourt Castle, where
we lived, was a retired British Army Officer, Hugh Hallinan,
and he, too, often invited me to fish salmon on a beat that
had been in his family for generations on the (southern)
Blackwater River in County Cork, downstream a few miles
from Fermoy. His beat was only about thirty feet long, and
next door to the Duke of Devonshire's famous fishery, one
of the finest stretches of salmon water in Western Europe.
Hugh's little beat was so narrow that only one of us could
fish it at a time, but it was gorgeously productive. The only
drawback was that if you hooked a salmon that wanted to
work downstream into the Duke's water, you couldn't work
down the shore with your fish, not because the Duke for-
bade us but because a gully separated the two beats. We lost
as many salmon into the Duke's water as we beached
ourselves.

Perhaps the finest sport of all was on a short stretch of
water — barely 300 yards between two weirs — on a historic
beat known as "The Mollies" on the (northern) Blackwater, a

bit upstream from where it joins the famous River Boyne, just outside the town of Navan and barely forty-five minutes easy drive from Dublin.

"The Mollies" was a beat that was held by a syndicate for many decades and, fortunately for me, the family of a good friend of mine in Dublin had been a member of the syndicate for generations. The family, the Luces, were academics, and they had "The Mollies" on Fridays. The father, Arthur Aston Luce, was Berkeley professor emeritus of moral philosophy at Trinity College Dublin, the Elizabethan academic twin of Oxford and Cambridge, and he had written a profound philosophical work, *Fishing and Thinking,* based on his experiences on "The Mollies," where he was still pursuing salmon into his eighties. He was Samuel Beckett's tutor at Trinity and had a great influence on the playwright — as well as on the salmon.

It was his son John, a senior fellow in classics at Trinity College, who was my friend, and who used to take me on occasional Fridays up to "The Mollies." The salmon there ran big, as big as those that come up the Boyne — fifteen-pounders and more. With John, I also fished for salmon and trout on the Newport and Westport Rivers out in the west, in Connemara, and we "dapped the mayfly" in Lough Corrib and Lough Sheelin.

If I came home with a good catch of salmon, I would cut a few steaks for broiling, set aside a half salmon for boiling and to eat cold with mayonnaise, and I would take any remaining salmon down to central Dublin to have smoked. In their peculiar way, the Irish insisted that they didn't know how to smoke salmon properly, and they used to ship their fish over to Dundee for smoking. But I found a fishmonger in the little Jewish shopping area of Clanbrassil Street who could smoke as well as anyone in Dundee and, what is more, he would keep "bank" for me. What to do with twenty pounds of fine Irish smoked salmon? I would take out, say, five pounds, and he would give me a "credit" for the remaining fifteen, upon which I would draw over the next few weeks; he would be selling in his store my freshly smoked salmon and I would be drawing salmon subsequently smoked by him on my "credit" as the weeks went by. In this way, during the salmon season and beyond, there was almost always a generous supply in our flat in Simmonscourt Castle. This was doubtless the reason for our popularity among certain members of the Abbey and Gayety theatre troupes, who loved to drop by for a plate of smoked salmon, a slice of Irish soda bread and a jar or three of (Foreign) Guinness stout.

Entitled to diplomatic privileges, I used to be able to obtain the extra-strength Foreign from Guinness out of bond. The locals could never get this cherished brew; they claimed that the difference between what they drank in the pubs and what I was able to serve them was like skimmed milk compared with whipping cream.

During my three years in Dublin, I was a member of the Dublin Salmon Anglers' Association, whose water was a stretch of the Liffey River in the heart of Dublin that wasn't highly productive, but it occasionally produced some big fish and had the advantage of opening on January 1; only one other river in Ireland, far out in Donegal, opened that early, while most other Irish salmon rivers opened in February or March.

On Opening Day a few members would brave the damp, near-freezing cold, in the hope of catching a salmon to enable the Association to make its traditional present of a fine fresh fish to the president of the Republic; the president's official residence, *Aras an Uachtarain*, was in Phoenix Park, not far from the Club's most productive Liffey beat. The members always hoped that I would produce a salmon on Opening Day; they knew that I would have to leave the river early in order to go home and change from waders into morning coat and striped trousers to attend, at noon, the president's New Year's Day levee for the diplomatic corps. Regretfully, for the levees that I attended, I never had a wet, wriggling Liffey salmon to present to President De Valera.

I was not unhappy at never having been invited by the

Guinness family or the Duke of Devonshire to fish their famous and productive waters. They, as well as lesser breeds in Ireland with riparian rights on salmon streams, might indeed invite you to fish, but they invoked the peculiar practice of immediately relieving you of your catch and shipping it into the Dublin morning fish auction.

Nor did I mind, after the trout and salmon season had closed, causing raised eyebrows among certain angling snobs by indulging in what they called "coarse" fishing, not for the enormous pike or bream to be found in many Irish rivers, but for fish in salt water. As a veteran surfcaster I found this sport virtually unknown in Ireland but, after some experimentation, I found that in some Irish areas it could be as exciting as on the south shore of Long Island or out on Cape Cod.

For example, along the east coast of Ireland, running south from Dublin, I could find excellent sole and other flat species. I shall always remember one freezing morning when, fishing from the beach at Greystones, in my chest waders, three sweaters, a heavy woollen shirt, hood and rain gear, and wondering why I was mad enough to suffer the damp cold, I saw an elderly woman emerge barefoot in a bathrobe from her cottage down the beach, stride across the sand to the water-line, throw off her robe and plunge into the freezing water. She assured me afterward that she took "her bath" every morning of the year.

This reminded me of the first swim I took out at the "Forty Foot" — a famous, voluntarily maintained swimming club at Sandycove, in the outskirts of Dublin, frequented by Irish playwrights, priests and poets, taking their daily "bath" in the nude. The "Forty-Foot" is the secluded swimming hole alongside the Martello Tower, immortalized by James Joyce in the opening paragraphs of *Ulysses*. When I entered, I asked one oldtimer what the water temperature was, and he replied: "Och, it's up to 50 and there ain't no bite in it."

I surprised George Burrows and other angling friends by showing them that tope could be taken casting into the surf from the shore. I found that I could hook this tough member of the shark family along the coast, using my North American surfcasting tackle for fifteen- to thirty-pound fish.

Anglers I met along the Irish coastline were a different breed from the salmon and trout fishermen. Through the winter months, for two years, I fished with a couple of rugged characters who didn't own a car but knew the coast so intimately, and refrained from discussing politics so assiduously, that I began to suspect that they were members of the IRA. One Saturday, while I was out fishing with George Burrows, my wife found herself coping with a Canadian alcoholic who had been poured off the Liverpool-Dublin ferry without a penny to his name. Not being able for the moment to reach our consular clerk, who dealt with such cases, Crenia found to her surprise that there was an AA listing in the Dublin telephone directory. Meanwhile, I got home just in time to see the AA car pull up. Out stepped two familiar characters — of all people, my two "IRA" shorefishing cronies — who turned out to be the Dublin reps of Alcoholics Anonymous.

Even more surprising than surfcasting for tope was to find that striped bass — yes, the genuine Cape Cod–Montauk Point striper — abounded in certain Irish waters. Most Irish angling friends thought me quite mad when I said I was going out for striped bass at the southeastern tip of Ireland, in a shoal area off the town of Rosslare, known as Splaugh Rock.

But locate stripers I did indeed — not Montauk Point or Cuttyhunk forty-pounders, but lots of "schoolies" in the five- to ten-pound range and, of course, fine sport and delicious eating. Before leaving Ireland I talked to people at Bord Failte — the excellent Irish Tourist Bureau — to tell them they had a wonderful attraction for North American fishermen, if only they would make it known. I doubt if one Irish fisherman in a thousand, to this day, knows what sport he can find in those waters off Rosslare, and possibly along other sections of the Irish coastline.

I can think of only one occasion when I really exploited my position in External in the interests of fishing — and it yielded the greatest freshwater fishing experience of my lifetime.

During 1954-55, I was U.S. desk officer and was working on the St. Lawrence seaway and power negotiations. It was apparent that the main new factor making the St. Lawrence seaway and power project feasible was the expected traffic of iron ore from the Knob Lake (Shefferville) area of Labrador into North America's industrial heartland. With a little strategy and a lot of luck, I got an invitation from the general manager of the Iron Ore Company to visit Knob Lake. But there were other things on my mind besides looking at strip mining for iron ore. I casually mentioned that I would bring a rod along, on the off-chance that I might find a moment to wet a line while up at Knob Lake. He must have "gotten the message." We took the train together from Montreal to Rimouski; flew across the St. Lawrence to Sept-Isles in a company plane; and did a little fishing in the St. Lawrence where I surprised the locals by taking codfish in the five- to ten-pound range by spincasting and flycasting.

Up at Knob Lake I soon learned that the message must indeed have been passed along. A couple of Iron Ore Co. executives volunteered to show me the mining operation the first day and to take me fishing the next three — if I had no objections! They seemed no less delighted than I with their "assignment." On our first day, we jeeped through the bush for a full two hours, passing dozens of gorgeous-looking and apparently virgin lakes and rivers but, as always, the best fishing is at least an hour or two away from wherever you are.

On the way they had mentioned that, since it was Thursday, everyone in Catholic Knob Lake would be wanting fish to eat the next day and would be hoping that we would bring back plenty for their larder. Notwithstanding, my companions said they would maintain their own ground rule — to release all speckled trout under two pounds. As I had never before caught a speckled trout weighing two pounds, I assumed they were kidding the "townie." They weren't.

When we finally arrived at *the* lake, they started me casting from shore, in hip waders, at the mouth of a "drainage," into limpid, fast-flowing water no more than two to three feet deep. I started with a No. 8 fly rod and a three-fly cast. First cast with the three flies — two trout. Second cast — one trout. Third cast — they broke me. New three-cast tippet — two trout. Then, broken again.

I was so excited that I hadn't noticed that the boys were putting most of my fish back, because they weighed "only" around two pounds. I switched to a leader with one fly and was taking three- and four- and five-pound wild, native speckled trout — fabulously coloured, immensely vigorous in the cold water, and altogether glorious. If anyone had offered me a wad of travellers' cheques and a flight for a holiday on, say, the French Riviera, I would have laughed in his face. Then, for no apparent reason, my companions said it was time to move.

In some new water a few minutes away, they suggested I put on a six-pound test tippet and a larger single fly. Within moments I was into an eight-pound ouananiche — a land-locked salmon — and it was the supreme thrill of all the years of fresh and salt water angling I had done. Later, my new friends suggested I change to a streamer and, flycasting along the shore, I began hitting grey trout in the five- to ten-pound range.

At still another spot, standing in a foot of smooth-flowing water and casting into no more than a three-foot depth, I hit more ouananiche, and speckled trout up to five pounds. And at another place, I was actually scared at the size and power of the Northern pike that broke me.

No trolling, no hardware or bait, no fumes from an outboard, no bush behind to foul backcasts. Just glorious, clean flycasting, into limpid, virgin waters — wading and thus fighting a fish in its own environment, on your own feet. Exquisite is the only word for that glorious Labrador experience. I've never had anything like it — before or since.

In Mexico, my ambassador, who claimed he enjoyed wetting a line, saw to it that during an official visit we made together up the west coast, we allowed ourselves time to accept invitations to go offshore in the Pacific or the Gulf of California for big game fishing. I took my first striped marlin and sailfish going out of Acapulco, Mazatlan, Guaymas, Topolobampo and La Paz, at the foot of Baja California. To be honest, however, I never did learn to enjoy this. Big game fishing is hour after hour of trolling, with the captain and mate doing everything — exercising *their* skill to locate, attract and hook the fish — while you sit strapped in a chair, with heavy tackle, and then heave and heave until your arms are ready to break and until the mate finally gaffs the monster you've brought alongside. In later years, I was invited to go fishing for big billfish out of Santa Marta, Baranquilla and Cartagena in Colombia, and out of Salinas and Guayaquil in Ecuador. I would accept an invitation only if it was agreed that I could use light tackle and troll or cast feathers preferably for that great game fish, the dolphin — not the mammal of the marine circuses but the multicoloured snubnosed *Coryphaena hippurus* that changes colour after coming out of the water. I never did manage to capture the famous *pez gallo* — roosterfish — along the Ecuadorian coast on the Pacific, nor to hit a wahoo off Santa Marta on Colombia's Caribbean Coast.

The equator lies just a couple of hundred miles south of Bogota, and the last thing I expected to do in that part of the world, where I served my final tour of duty as ambassador before retiring, was fly fishing for trout. I soon discovered that I had quite respectable rainbow trout fishing — the whole year around and with no closed season — within an hour's easy drive from our official residence in Bogota, at Lake Neusa at 10,000 feet altitude. In Ecuador, through which the equator runs, I have flycast in lakes up to 15,000 feet.

The secret, of course, is altitude. It governs every aspect of your daily life in the Andean tropics. Rainbow trout can thrive the year round in the tropics — at around 7,000 feet, and above. The U.S. Fish and Wildlife Service — in one of the earliest and most useful examples of what today we call technical assistance to lesser-developed countries — carried out a rainbow trout stocking program throughout the High Andes, from Mexico to Tierra del Fuego. (For stocking, they used Canadian Rocky Mountain rainbows, which they figured would be the most adaptable to the altitude of the High Andes.) In some places — for example, in Lake Titicaca at 12,000 feet, between Bolivia and Peru; in Lake Tota at 9,000 feet in Northern Colombia; and in most of the rivers in Tierra del Fuego — the rainbows run to enormous size, equalling the biggest steelheads of British Columbia and the exciting new runs in the Great Lakes. My Saturday morning flycasting in Lake Neusa was for much more modest fish; my best rainbow trout there, on the fly, ran just over four pounds.

I pursued the elusive and wily snook and rugged, leaping tarpon in the inshore and brackish waters of Mexico and Colombia. Both are magnificent game fish that readily take the fly — but much larger flies than you would ever use back home for salmon or Great Northern pike.

Quite the wildest fishing expedition I ever made in Latin America was with Nick Covasavic, head of Goodrich Euzkadi de Mexico. This was to seek rainbows planted by the U.S. Fish and Wildlife Service in a lake of melted snow in the crater of an extinct volcano, the 15,000-foot Nevada de Toluca, a half-hour's drive west of Mexico City. A "road" wound only part way up the mountain, but Nick figured, "If those fellows could get to the top to plant trout, we can get up there to catch them."

With the ruggedest four-wheel-drive vehicle that Nick could commandeer at Goodrich, we easily went half way up the Nevada. When the "road" came to an end, we worked our way along a narrow, pre-Colombian, cobblestone path, and when that too gave out we slowly drove on through brush and cactus in ever-diminishing circles around and up the mountain. Every so often large rocks from the slopes above tumbled down with frightening momentum, but we dodged them all. At 14,000 feet on our altimeter, we came across a chap sitting in the grass and staring into space. He looked kind of lost or weird, and we wondered if he was on drugs; but he turned out to be a Connecticut entomologist studying insect life at high altitude. We said we were there to fish. He had just discovered that there was no insect or crustacean life at that altitude. *He* thought *us* quite mad.

We crossed the rim of the Nevada's crater at just under 15,000 feet and descended the smooth lava slope of the crater to the water's edge. We started casting spinners into crystal-clear water and, with our Polaroids, could see trout at the maximum distance of our cast. We hooked a couple of fish to prove to ourselves that it could be done at those heights, in the apparently complete absence of aquatic insect or other marine life, and made our hazardous return journey down the Nevada and back to Mexico City.

My only disappointing postings, piscatorially speaking, were in Ottawa, a poor relation of Ontario's Ministry of Natural Resources, and Uruguay. It was not that Uruguay did not offer good sport. The prized *dorado*, a great freshwater game fish, attracts many anglers to the upper basins of the Parana and Paraguay Rivers. The bluefish run to record size along the shoreline of the Plata estuary around Punta del Este and beyond. The trouble was that six weeks after we arrived in Uruguay Mr Trudeau ordered closure of our mission in Montevideo. This can be one of the more traumatic experiences for a Head of Post, and in those unhappy circumstances I didn't seek solace in fishing.

While surfcasting on the Mexican shore between Acapulco and Zijuatanejo, in Colombia between Cartagena and Santa Marta, and in Ecuador between Salinas and Guayaquil, I would sometimes find youngsters on the beach with monofilament lines, hooks and sinkers, attempting to throw

their rig out into the surf, not for the sport but to catch
something for the family dinner.

Their method was primitive. Each lad would coil his line
on the sand, grip it a few feet behind the sinker and hook,
swing it a few times around his head and let fly. They would
look with envy at my surfcasting tackle and the distance I
could cast with it; in fishing the surf, every extra yard you
can cast often improves the catch exponentially.

So I showed them how they could increase casting dis-
tances easily and, most important, without a penny's
expense — by adapting the principle of the spinning reel to
what they had at hand.

Spinning is slip-casting, from a stationary spool. The line
slips off the spool — and it can just as easily slip off a tin can,
pop bottle or glass jar.

I showed the youngsters that by winding their monofilament lines on a can, and then swinging the end of their lines,
with sinker, around their heads, exactly as they were
accustomed to doing, and turning the can towards the water
as they let go, the line would slip off and out much more
smoothly. (Casting a line that is coiled on the sand makes it
start out with a jerk, with friction from the sand and with
tangles and frustration.)

I was sometimes able to increase a youngster's cast by a
few yards, after only a few moments instruction, utilizing an
old can or bottle found on the beach. I will never forget the
look of amazement and sheer joy of a lad I had been instructing on the Ecuadorian shoreline north of Guayaquil. Slipcast-
ing from a tin can we found on the beach, he was soon able
to cast his sinker and bait a few yards farther out in the surf
than he had been able to reach before. All of a sudden he
hooked into a snook — a five-pound beauty, which took a
leap into the sun. But he held on and, ten minutes later, he
brought it wriggling onto the beach. The snook is a great
game and a fine eating fish — always expensive in the
marketplace. He dashed off proudly to show his prize to his
no-doubt hungry family.

I have often thought this simple shore-line instruction would make a useful, costless "technical-assistance" project to aid developing countries — frequenting tropical beaches and demonstrating the principle and practice of "slip-casting" to increase the yield from the restless, pounding, bountiful surf.

My world's record catch? Glad you reminded me. After retiring, Crenia and I began to spend winters in Florida, where I fished no more than thirty mornings a month, for four months each winter. I did a bit of trailblazing by using fly tackle in pursuit of sea trout and redfish (a first cousin of the striped bass farther north) which are to be found in the brackish water (half-salt, half-sweet) of the Indian and Banana Rivers of the Intercoastal Waterway, and other inshore waters. Down there, not one fisherman in a thousand was using fly tackle. Many Canadian snowbirds would say: "We didn't dream you could use fly tackle for this type of fishing. Must remember to bring it with us next winter."

In the winter of 1984, on the morning of March 5 to be exact, I was flycasting in a favourite stretch of water, about two feet or less in depth, on the Indian River flats just behind Sebastian Inlet. I was just about to stop and return home, and I gave "one last cast." I hit a 12½ lb. sea trout, which turned out to be a couple of pounds heavier than the pre-existing world's record fish of that species caught on a fly. My record, awarded by the International Game Fish Association, still stands.

P.S. As I said somewhere above, thank goodness I had the reputation of being a dedicated and hard-working member of the Canadian foreign service.

For the
Uninitiated

Our Valiant
Consuls

Walking into our chancery one day in Bogota, I said good morning to a girl in the reading room, with a Vancouver paper in her lap, and asked if she was being looked after and whether she had some problem.

"Do I ever," she burst out. "Yesterday my purse was snatched, with money, ticket home, passport, everything. I've travelled nearly all over South America, even hitchhiking. I know how to take care of myself and how to hang on to my bag. But here in Bogota, for the first time ever, they got it."

She was about twenty-one and seemed pretty street-smart. I remarked sympathetically that even in Mexico City, Bogota's thieves were conceded to be *Numero Uno* and I asked her how it happened (I thought I'd heard them all).

"I went out from my hotel to go window-shopping, carrying my bag in a way that always beats purse-snatchers," she said. "You know, at this altitude, it gets cold around sundown, and I had to find a washroom. I couldn't see a hotel or any other place to do it, but there was this park with bushes, across the road. I ducked into the bushes and while I was squatting, out comes this hand from nowhere, grabs my purse off the ground and he beats it."

After interviewing her and verifying her Canadian iden-
tity, our vice-consul suggested she phone collect from our
office to her family or friends, and ask them to have the
amount of money she needed transferred from their bank to
External in Ottawa, which would then wire our embassy
authority to give her the equivalent in local pesos. He issued
her a limited-validity passport and advanced her $35 for a
night at the hotel and a day's food. In his routine report, our

vice-consul noted that she was "robbed of purse during
moment of maximum vulnerability and immobility."

Although this happened in 1975, it will illustrate what
can happen during the 36 million trips which Canadians
currently make abroad each year — ranging from a day in
New York City to a few months in Kabul or Katmandu.
Assistance in some form can require our embassies and
consulates in foreign countries to handle around 650,000
requests per annum.

It is our consuls who give Canadians "protection and
assistance" — to use the official phrase — when they run
into difficulties abroad. We now have around 350 consular
officers in Canada's posts abroad, working in our embassies
in foreign capitals, or at our consulates in large cities outside
the capitals, such as Hamburg, New York, Marseilles, Milan,
Rio de Janeiro, or Glasgow. Most of our people doing diplomatic work have done the consular side at some time during

their career; some specialize in consular work most of their career.

Recession and depreciation of our dollar notwithstanding, the amount of foreign travel undertaken by peripatetic Canadians, the bizarre situations they find themselves in, or the plain misfortunes that befall them, is quite astonishing. Canadians are not used to riding camels, but can't resist doing so when visiting the Egyptian pyramids; and novices sometimes break a limb falling off the gentle beasts. Travellers not only lose their passports, but forget that their passports will expire while they are listening to Wagner's *Ring* at Bayreuth or making their expedition up Kilimanjaro. Pockets are picked, purses are snatched, and their cars crash. Some folks can't remember the name of the hotel they checked into before they quickly rushed out to the bullfight for the first *olé*. The moneyorder from father never seems to arrive on time. They get belligerent in Copenhagen's Tivoli Gardens or Dublin's Phoenix Park, find themselves unexpectedly broke in Bombay or Dar-es-Salaam, pregnant anywhere, separated from friends, in states of hallucination, or are just plain bewildered or bewitched.

A consul at our embassy in Athens was confronted by the problem of the lady from Winnipeg who had bought two, first-class, one-way tickets to Greece — one for herself and one for her dog, had checked into a luxurious hotel, hadn't emerged from her room for days until the management broke in and found she had $50 left in the world to pay her bill and return to Manitoba.

Our consul in Milan listened to an affluent Ontarian relate how he was sightseeing with his wife in their new Mercedes, which he was determined never to leave unguarded on the street for one moment. (He had heard that thievery of expensive foreign cars in that area was rife.) But his wife wanted to snap photos of a statue they were passing, so he told her to get out of the car while he sat in it at the curb, engine running. A small boy popped out of nowhere and urinated on the front fender. The irate Ontarian jumped out of the car, leaving the engine running and the door open, to chase the lad away. This took about ten seconds — sufficient for an accomplice to slip into the driver's seat and take off with one more "Ontario" Mercedes.

In Bogota, our consul, Jim Bartleman, had his own car stolen while he was standing next to it with his hand on the hood. He was driving in a heavy rain which obscured the house numbers on the street of a friend he was to pick up. With the motor running, he got out for a moment and walked around his car to the curb, to get a better look at a house number, and was startled to feel the car slide away from him as he was peering through the rain. And he was no less surprised a few days later at seeing a newspaper advertisement telling him that the car would be returned on payment of $1,000 and giving him an undertaking that it would not be "molested" again while he was still in the country.

In Ottawa, a routine report came in from our embassy in Spain telling of a retired Canadian who, after registering at a hotel in Madrid and leaving his baggage, identification and travellers' cheques in his hotel room, went out for dinner but could not find his way back to his hotel nor could he remember the name of the hotel. In spite of a thorough search of hotel directories by embassy staff and numerous inquiries over a period of two days by Spanish police and tourist officials, the name and address of the hotel could not be determined. Finally, one of the locally engaged staff and her boy-friend volunteered to drive the subject through the streets and, after four hours, the hotel was finally located. The subject's clothes and identification were found in his room. At Christmas, the embassy received a thank-you letter from the subject in Canada. Total number of hours spent on case: twenty.

Before the Argentinians were dislodged from the Falkland Islands after their 1982 invasion, they allowed radio-communication between a Canadian settler on the Islands and our consul in Buenos Aires, who had enquired about his welfare. The consul was startled to hear the request that he ask the Argentine authorities for help in capturing the settler's bull, which, in heat, had run away. The bull was never found, and the settler then asked for semen to be sent to him by the Department of Agriculture.

Our consul in New York interviewed a Canadian who had escaped from jail in Quebec and was mugged one night in Times Square. He was requesting repatriation with the argument that he would be safer in jail back home than on the streets of Manhattan.

In Mexico, our vice-consul went down to Vera Cruz to help a young girl from Calgary. She had been sitting in the railway station when a railway worker, having his siesta on a rafter above, rolled over in his sleep, fell into her lap and broke one of her arms and legs.

During one week of the high season for tourists in Mexico, our embassy's consular section was involved with a couple from Winnipeg and a Canadian admiral hunting for missing daughters; with two Montrealers in hospital after a bad car accident; with a Windsor student in jail for possessing hashish; with the murder of an Albertan couple living in retirement in Baja California; with repatriating two destitute Canadians back to their homes; and with visits to hospitals, jails, undertakers, police headquarters and whatnot.

This may not be the life of high diplomacy, but it is the nitty-gritty of the consular side of the foreign service, and can be a salutary experience for the exposure it provides to fellow Canadians. In this area of the work of the foreign service — protection and assistance to Canadians abroad — the human face of government is seen by the public. More often than not, the incidents produce stress; but few consuls who have aided or comforted a traveller who is ill, bereaved, jailed, destitute, victimized, threatened or emotionally disturbed, have remained unmoved by the experience. Never is the secretary of state for external affairs and the Department more open to praise — in the House of Commons or in the press — when consuls succeed in helping Canadians in trouble abroad, and never more vulnerable to blame if they fail.

A few heads-of-post abroad, in earlier years, resisted the assignment of women to consular work, questioning how effective women would be with jailers in Istanbul, police in Mexico City or customs officials in Riyadh. I will say simply that I wouldn't have traded Mary Stock, who served under me as vice-consul in Mexico City, or Rollande Vézina, our consul in Bogota, for anyone else.

Terrorism, etcetera

Luckily, Canada still ranks low on international terrorism's Hit List, but the Department of External Affairs spares no effort to minimize the risks to its foreign service personnel. They aren't exactly an endangered species, but work in some parts of the world may put them in one of our country's higher risk occupations.

One obvious hot spot during the past decade has been Iran. Jim George, Canadian ambassador to Iran in the late '70s, was startled one day when he phoned his office from home and heard a stranger cut in and say, "Mr George, I am going to kill you." Trying to remain calm, Jim asked who was speaking and what was his problem. The voice simply added, "Mr George, I am being paid to kill you."

From then on, Jim was guarded night and day until he was posted to another country. He learned that the threat to him was a matter of guilt by association: terrorist elements had been frustrated in their attempts to kidnap or assassinate the United States ambassador, a former head of the CIA, and had decided that Canada's man might be a suitable alternative. In 1980, then-Ambassador Kenneth Taylor and his staff had to flee Iran after helping six United States Embassy employees to escape. The Americans had been hiding in the Canadian staff quarters after the U.S. Embassy was seized by Iranian revolutionaries and its large staff held hostage (and then held for over a year). That was the episode that rocked Jimmy Carter's U.S. presidency.

More recently, our chargé d'affaires in Tehran was recalled for "consultations" in the world-wide uproar caused by the Ayatollah Ruhollah Khomeini's call for the assassination of British author Salman Rushdie, following publication of his book *The Satanic Verses*.

The rise of terrorism over the past two decades has caused security measures to be tightened at Canadian posts around the world. Staff heading off to foreign assignments are instructed in how to make themselves less predictable and less alluring as targets for gunmen and kidnappers.

Stenographers and clerks, as well as ambassadors and consuls general, are briefed on such undiplomatic surprises as personal safety, terrorist tactics (which may vary greatly in different parts of the world), evading pursuers, destroying documents, and the nuts and bolts of emergency communications.

Briefings are given on the political and security characteristics of the area to which a person is being posted, including the possible threat from political terrorists — or from ordinary criminals looking for profit from violence or blackmail. At the same time, to keep the threat to Canadians in realistic perspective, External Affairs stresses that the annual toll from terrorism is small when compared to the fatalities from traffic accidents in safer parts of the world.

If the Canadian foreign service has rarely been targetted by terrorists, Externalites nevertheless face an uncontrollable hazard — of finding themselves somewhere at the wrong time, or in the wrong place.

A striking example of this was the case of Robert Elliott, when he was Canada's ambassador to Egypt. He was seated in the reviewing stand near President Anwar Sadat to witness the 1980 military parade in the heart of Cairo. Some Moslem

fundamentalist soldiers, themselves marching in the
parade, broke ranks and sprayed the reviewing stand with a
hail of bullets. President Sadat, the acting Coptic pope and
other notables were slain. Miraculously, Elliott wasn't even
scratched. At his next post, Nigeria, his car was inexplicably
trashed by an ugly mob while he was being driven to the
airport of Benim.

A couple of years later, our counsellor in Ankara, Ted
Galpin, took his wife and daughter to the airport, bound for
London. Their flight was delayed and the airline manager
suggested they pass the time in the restaurant-lounge. Coming out of nowhere, two Armenians opened fire with
machine guns and sprayed the crowded check-in area the
Galpins had just left. The Galpins ducked under a table, just
as one of the terrorists entered the restaurant-lounge with
the airline manager in tow as a hostage. The Galpin family
managed to remain hidden during the three-hour ordeal,
during which the terrorists shot and killed a dozen persons,
including the airline manager and a restless American
woman, and wounded seventy others. Galpin recalled that
while they sweated under the table, the airport Muzak kept
playing "Auld Lang Syne."

In 1976, when Lebanon's civil war rose to one of its many
fever pitches, External Affairs closed its embassy in Beirut
and transferred its operations to neighbouring and hitherto
peaceful Amman, the capital of Jordan. A few months later,
External received the following message from Amman:

> Singleton and Vézina were the only staff in the Canadian
> offices at the start of the attack around 9h45. With bullets
> flying through the windows and the sound of machine-
> gun fire inside the hotel creeping ever closer to the office,
> Singleton took refuge in his office's bathroom, and even-
> tually in the bath. Ms Vézina also found safe hiding in her
> office's bathroom where she spent more than two hours
> along with three consular visitors and two hotel
> employees. Unable to communicate with Ms Vézina and

feeling the going rather hot, Singleton crawled out of a window, scampered across a rooftop and slid down a drainpipe to the ground and safety. As for Ms Vézina's group, around 12h15 they were summoned out of the bathroom with their hands up by Jordanian troops and marched to an army post from which they were promptly released. The situation is back to normal and staff have re-occupied the battle-scarred premises.

This telegram to Ottawa was repeated to Washington, from which Singleton received a telegram signed by some well-wishing friends. It read: "Appalled to learn of attempt on your position and person. Grateful advise if bathtub was filled and how far down the drain you went."

Examples of "near misses" abound in External's files. Only a last-minute change of flight plans saved Canadian diplomatic couriers from travelling on the fatal Air India flight, and on the Egyptair plane that was highjacked to Malta in 1985 and liberated only with heavy loss of life, including a Canadian mother and child.

My successor as ambassador in Bogota was delayed a half hour in leaving our embassy to attend a National Day reception at the embassy of the Dominican Republic. But during that half hour, "M-19" guerrillas stormed and occupied the Dominican Embassy, seizing the Papal nuncio (now nuncio in Ottawa), several supreme court justices and cabinet ministers, and two dozen assorted ambassadors (from countries with which the "M-19" had no quarrel whatsoever). They let everyone go in stages except the ambassadors, whom they held in the embassy for two months, and finally released them in Havana.

In Malaysia a Japanese Red Army hit-squad shot up the Japanese Embassy in a downtown Kuala Lumpur building. The Canadian Embassy staff held their breath and counted the minutes — in their office one floor below.

From the examples above, it will be obvious that Canadian foreign service personnel not only have to take into account where they work and play but also the company they keep. I had a vivid demonstration of this back in 1969, when I was serving as Canadian head of mission in Montevideo.

The United States Ambassador, Robert Sayre, knew I was a keen angler and he invited me to go fishing one Sunday morning. (This was at a time when the Tupamaros, Latin America's earliest urban guerrillas, were shifting their tactics from non-violent, Robin-Hood-type derring-do to terrorism.) The ambassador's invitation was to fish in the Plata River, from a friend's yacht docked about a half-hour's drive upstream from the Uruguayan capital.

I drove to the marina alone, in my own car. Mr Sayre was driven up with bodyguards in a bullet-proof vehicle, with a U.S. Embassy lead car and follow car, each of which was led and followed by jeeps with Uruguayan soldiers armed to the teeth. While we were fishing, Uruguayan military helicopters droned overhead. It resembled a scene right out of the Costa-Gavras film Z.

The Tupamaros did not bother us that day; they were busy planning the kidnapping of British Ambassador Geoffrey Jackson (who had previously been British trade commissioner in Toronto); he was kidnapped a few days later on a street close to the Canadian Embassy, and held for a year in a Tupamaro "People's Prison."

Occasionally, Canadian foreign service persons — of any rank — may find themselves exposed to another type of hazard, not created by foreign terrorists but by disgruntled Canadian citizens. Our embassies and consulates abroad not unreasonably seem to epitomize, in the minds of some travelling Canadians, the totality of the federal government and its bureaucracy in Ottawa and the authorities in the capital of their own provinces. Our posts occasionally find themselves targetted by a travelling compatriot seeking to vent his spleen "against the government" — as happened dramatically back in February 1976, in Beirut, Lebanon, where Alan Sullivan was serving as chargé d'affaires of the Canadian Embassy.

At that time, a Canadian citizen of Lebanese origin, whom I shall call Eddie, was having a protracted dispute with some authorities of his home province, British Columbia, to build a sort of "castle" on an island in the middle of Okanagan Lake. In addition, he was involved in a contentious child-custody wrangle with his Canadian wife. Both of these matters brought him to our embassy on the numerous occasions when he was visiting Beirut.

One morning Eddie, and several Lebanese friends armed to the teeth, erupted within the embassy and held Alan Sullivan and his staff at gunpoint for nearly six hours. They listened nervously as Eddie vented his frustrations with Canada generally, British Columbia particularly, and his wife especially. Sullivan finally managed to talk Eddie into a state of quiescence — and to free the embassy. As Alan said, there was already enough turbulence in Lebanon because of its catastrophic civil war and he didn't need this extra anxiety! The embassy closed later that year — for reasons of violence unconnected to Eddie and his family.

However much diplomatic immunity may be disregarded today, it is one of the oldest and *was* one of the most widely recognized rules of customary international law. For two millennia it had been accepted that to perform their most elementary functions — presenting their government's policies to the receiving state and reporting on the latter's views back home — the persons, premises, facilities and movements of diplomats must reciprocally be considered sacrosant. As an Alberta University law professor, Leslie Green, has noted:

> The diplomatic carriers of messages from one Greek City State to another were considered to be under the protection of the gods; so generally recognized was their immunity that, even though they might have been instructed to present a declaration of war they were able to return home unscathed, even if hostilities had already broken out.

How the times have changed!

The Queen's English
(and Other Matters)

Although I have done a fair amount of writing and editing during active service in External and in retirement, I confess that I never saw anything resembling a departmental manual or style book in English usage. At the most, some Division head might issue some do's and dont's, ephemeral pieces of paper that would usually disappear when the issuing zealot moved on.

In my earlier years in External, in the late '40s and throughout the '50s, departmental effort seemed to be devoted as much to destroying writing style as to improving it. This resulted partly from External's continuing preoccupation with minimizing expense and labour in its growing telegram traffic. For decades, its facilities for enciphering, deciphering, transmitting, or receiving messages were puny, compared to the sophisticated and globe-encircling telegraphic facilities it enjoys today. In earlier years, a month never went by without an edict from On High enjoining us to cut, abbreviate or dispense entirely with our precious telegrams. Letters and despatches sent by diplomatic bag or, if they were not sensitive in content, by mail, were encouraged, rather than costly telegrams. If telegrams really had to be sent, the priorities we assigned

179

to them (flash, most urgent, immediate, etc.) were rigor-
ously monitored.

Occasionally a prize would be offered for traffic-cutting
suggestions. I did *not* win one when, to illustrate how a
journalist intending to resign might compress words and
send a message that read UPSHOVE JOB ASSWARDS —
incurring cable charges for only three words instead of at
least six or seven sentences, paragraphs, or pages.

But the telegram-paring fanatics found it difficult to cope,
as their successors doubtless do today, with certain Externally human failings: the higher the rank, the more marked
the propensity of officers to send their reports by cable
rather than by mail or diplomatic bag. An imposing list of
addressees (prime minister, minister, under-secretary, etc.)
and a high security classification (preferably Top Secret:
Canadian Eyes Only) would also more likely catch the eye of
their betters at headquarters than a letter sent by slower
diplomatic bag and with a low security classification like
"Confidential."

In 1952, I was appointed External's official spokesman
and head of its puny Press Office (consisting of myself and a
clerk). I soon found that the prevailing mentality in External
Affairs was that the best way to guard its secrets — which
included about everything the Department did at that time,
no matter how innocuous — was to keep the spokesman/
press officer in total ignorance, at least until some public
announcement unhappily could no longer be avoided.

So I sought to convince the under-secretary, Arnold
Heeney, that the best way to guard the Department's secrets
was to make me privy to them. If I, External's spokesman,
were kept in ignorance, the press would seek out other
officers perhaps less qualified in dealing with the press;
whereas, if I were kept informed about what the hell was
going on, I could anticipate questions that might arise,
answers that could be given, responses that might be
expected, and problems that could otherwise not be
avoided.

This wise and quite novel idea was quickly approved by the discerning Mr Heeney and I began to receive the Department's daily "pack" of telegrams, which required three to four hours to read. I then proposed that I also be provided with copies of memos to the minister, which would provide exposure to the whole spectrum of External's activities, normally available only to the under-secretarial group. Mr Heeney again agreed with this wisdom, but I ran into an awkward problem: how stenos could squeeze out an extra carbon copy for me in addition to the half dozen required for the top hierarchy. Your place in the pecking order of External could be unerringly discerned from the legibility of the carbon copy you received of a memo to the minister. My ambitious and revolutionary program of self-education nearly foundered over the stenographers' difficulty in producing for me a legible seventh carbon copy. (A thick vellum original was mandatory for memos for the minister.)

I soon required my first reading glasses. This will explain my odd conviction that the modern photocopy machine, not the computer, is the most important technological breakthrough since sliced bread. Today's coddled Externalites would not find credible what we had to do to manage without it, and without word processors or facsimile machines.

But those early East Block days could provide a wondrous linguistic bounty to anyone who took the trouble to profit from it — an exposure to distinguished colleagues who could write the Queen's English with elegance and style: Charles Ritchie, John Holmes, Escott Reid, Mike Pearson, Hume Wrong, Herbert Norman, and the quite extraordinary Archibald A. Day. It was not so much that these exalted officers sought to teach you but, if you had any interest in matters of language, you could not help but learn from them — if only by proximity and a little osmosis. And they *would* take the trouble to be helpful, because in earlier days the quality of our writing was considered important.

Some of our learning came through enjoinders to observe

their pet taboos. In 1950, John Holmes descended on us at Canada's Permanent Mission to the United Nations in New York and promptly asserted that Externalites do NOT feel; they *think* such-and-such, or *believe*, or *hold the view* that, or *are of the opinion*...John did NOT report to Ottawa that he felt that the United States would support Canada's draft; rather, he *believed* that the U.S. would. He *thought* that our draft might command a majority, although the French delegate *held the view* that we might fail. There was this and so much more to learn from John if you would only take the trouble. After all, he went on to become Canada's foremost expositor of our foreign policy and international relations. Except to the denser among us, John Holmes's impeccable crafting on pieces of paper was infectious.

Deputy Under-Secretary Escott Reid, you would quickly learn, disliked sentences starting with "however," was unhappy with mixed metaphors such as "kindle a seed," and abhorred the use of unwarranted verbs — however conventional they might be — in place of some form of the simple "to be," such as "this figure *represents* a fifty percent increase in Canada's exports," or "wheat *emerged* as the leading component in our balance of payments."

And then there was Assistant Under-Secretary Charles Ritchie. I saw little of his writing; perhaps even then he was secreting it for his wonderful diaries. But what he did to our paperwork, or at least mine! He could drive you up the wall with obscure comments on your precious memo, and wrote seemingly in hieroglyphics. Down the left-hand margin of your memo, he might simply draw a wavy, vague line, leaving you to wonder what on earth he meant by it. At the end of some paragraph, he might inscribe an enigmatic "Really?" or and equally unhelpful "Mmm." To precipitate under-secretarial decision-making, you would conclude your memo by offering a couple of mutually exclusive options for approval or disapproval. Charles, bless his soul, would scribble after the *two* of them "Yes," or "Agreed."

Indisputably External's most ardent, most untiring, early

champion of good English was that erudite stylist, Archibald
A. Day. Archie had been a classics scholar at Queen's University, and he had a wide knowledge of literature and the
humanities. From 1949 to 1951, he had been seconded from
External to serve as secretary of the Royal Commission on
National Development in the Arts, Letters and Sciences (the
famed Massey Commission) and wrote much of its path-
breaking report. I began to work under Archie when he was
appointed head of the Department's omnibus Information
Division, which had been enlarged to absorb some journalistic types (including myself) from the terminating Wartime
Information Board.

When I began working for Archie in 1951, he had become
appalled at the bureaucratese, if not plain functional illit-
eracy, that he had found around External, notwithstanding
the superb English written by some illustrious colleagues. He
soon issued three memoranda on "The Queen's English,"
which were not simply *obiter dicta* on linguistic malprac-
tices around the East Block and the Daly Building and the
other structural excrescences amongst which Externalites
were scattered in those years; they were Delphic Oracles on
style, composition and usage. I still have his revised version,
issued in 1956, when he was appointed head of Consular
Division, where he became even more appalled, if that were
possible, at the blemishes in the *belles-lettres* with which he
was presented for signature.

In his memoranda Archie inveighed, for example, against
the misuse of "advise" when "inform" was intended: the
under-secretary *informed* the minister that he would be
taking his vacation in July and *advised* the minister not to
appoint an acting under-secretary during that month. Advise
means to give advice, Archie insisted, and not to give information. (So wide-spread has this misusage become that its
sanction has crept, shockingly, into the *Concise Oxford* and
Roget's Thesaurus.)

Archie would not tolerate "ongoing" (for continuing),
"upcoming" (for impending or soon), "overall" (which

means an article of clothing) or the barbaric practice of using a noun as a verb ("to impact on the Treasury"). Nor would he tolerate, especially at the beginning of a sentence, phrases like "in regard to," "in connection with," "in this connection"; these he denigrated usually as unnecessary — the writer's equivalent of a speaker clearing his throat or as hack filler-phrases, "most of them meaningless and time-consuming," which have "crept treacherously into External's correspondence."

A favourite Archie Day bugaboo was the misplacement of "only " when used as an adverb or adjective. It cannot be rammed into a sentence anywhere, he said, and should be used to limit only the word or phrase it immediately precedes (or follows). Archie rebuked Consular Division for writing "Passports are only issued to authorized holders." That suggests, he said, that External confines itself to issuing passports, not to ramming them down people's throats or distributing them as presents. The sentence, of course, should read "Passports are issued only to authorized persons."

I would add that correct placement of "only" will avoid ambiguity or downright error. Consider "I only want a glass of beer." Does this mean I don't crave a glass of beer but just want it? Does it mean I don't want Scotch, just beer? Does it mean I don't want a whole jug but just a glass?

Surprisingly, for the head of Consular Division, Archie did not pounce on the common misuse of immigrate and emigrate. (Albert Einstein emigrated from Britain; he emigrated to the United States, where he became an immigrant.)

In 1985, Canada's Department of the Secretary of State published a rather pompously entitled but highly useful volume, *The Canadian Style: A Guide to Writing and Editing*. But even this volume, if Archie were alive to see it, would not be found without blemish. Its very first sentence starts: "The Department of the Secretary of State's Translation Bureau is pleased to present..." Now read what Archie Day had to say in "The Queen's English" in 1956:

PLEASED — The expressions "we are pleased to advise you that" and "I shall be pleased to refer this matter…" occur repeatedly in our correspondence. As for the first phrase, if it is going to be used, why not complete it so it will read "we are graciously pleased to advise you that"? "We are pleased" is suitable for the style of a reigning monarch, and the use of the plural "We" adds to the pomposity of this bit of jargon. "We" may very properly be used, of course, when it is thought necessary to imply that the decision has been reached through departmental consultation; most of our letters are signed by or for the under-secretary or the minister, so that the singular pronoun "I" is normally appropriate. It is strongly recommended that the whole business of "pleased to advise," whether plural or singular, be abandoned, and that it be replaced by some such simple phrase as: "I am now able to inform you that…"

Archie could not tolerate a phase like "I shall not fail to let you know." He said: "This equally pompous expression occurs with painful frequency in our correspondence. This is a heavy and melodramatic way of saying: 'I shall let you know promptly'. The implication of this high-voltage phrase is that, 'Come earthquake or revolution, come tempest, flood or pestilence, I shall somehow manage to struggle to my office in the Daly Building and let you know that there has been no change as yet in the Immigration regulations'."

I could go on. You will realize, of course, that Archie's memoranda, and *The Canadian Style*, however valuable they may be in reducing your errors and other gaucheries, will not really help you acquire elegance of style and felicity of expression — in the manner of a John Holmes or a Harold Nicholson.

The new State volume will indeed help you correctly and uniformly to abbreviate, hyphenate, capitalize, spell, punctuate, italicize, quote, proofread and index (there are chapters on all these) and there is an especially useful appendix,

"Elimination of sexual, racist and ethnic stereotyping in written communications." The book is also useful because it reminds us when to use continual rather than continuous, to avoid defective when you mean deficient, to distinguish compare from contrast and characteristic from typical. Of course, we all know the difference between appraise and apprise, liable and likely, allusion and illusion, assume and presume, fewer and less, farther and further, etcetera, etcetera.

Joining Up —
and Surviving

To enter External you need a college degree —
if you aspire to officer rank — and you must compete
successfully in written and oral examinations, conducted
annually by External Affairs and the Public Service Commission in various parts of Canada and at some centres abroad.
Fluency in foreign languages, or a degree in political science
or international affairs, will be no guarantee of success; a
degree in classics, English literature, economics, engineering,
biology or history will do just as well — *if* you can pass the
government's examinations. They are prepared in such a
way as to enable persons of varying backgrounds but with
intelligence, imagination and the ability to write and articu-
late in English or French to compete on a level playing field.

In the British tradition, the Department has followed the
"generalist" approach in its personnel policy — in admitting,
training, assigning and posting its officers.

"Generalist" means that if you have been a good brick-
layer before admission, you will probably find yourself starting work as a plumber, and when you have mastered that
you may well find yourself turning to carpentry. In my own
career, for example, I entered External Affairs with seven
years of undergraduate and post-graduate study in eco-

nomics behind me, and my best foreign language was Italian. I never served in any division that dealt with international economic or financial matters, and I was never posted to Rome or Milan. Specialists on the Far East may find themselves dealing with Latin America, and Arabists may find themselves handling defence-related affairs. On balance — and of course there are pros and cons — it works. "Generalism" has been modified somewhat in recent years to permit career streaming — assignment to divisions in Ottawa and to posts abroad for specialists in politics, economics, commerce, aid and development and social affairs (immigration).

You can expect to spend about half your career in Ottawa and about half, or perhaps more, abroad — alternating between a couple of years at home and two to four years in one or other of 164 foreign posts, in sometimes dizzying succession. I never suffered "culture shock" going abroad, only on returning to Ottawa to find myself facing the rows of tired food in our government cafeteria, which is nevertheless considered to be the best of its kind in the capital city.

You are rarely given a repeat tour of duty at the same post, unless you rise to exalted ranks; not infrequently, an officer may be appointed ambassador to a country in which he has served some years back as a young third or second secretary. If you can climb the departmental ladder and are sent abroad to head a post, you will be dignified with the title of ambassador, high commissioner (same thing, but in Commonwealth countries) or consul general; when you come back to headquarters you may be a head of division, director general of a bureau or assistant under-secretary depending on your capabilities and experience. Personnel work in a ministry of foreign affairs is a challenging task, requiring a tough skin, a modicum of compassion, lots of imagination, and a talent for improvization. And choosing a person to head Personnel may require a talent for star-gazing.

Before seeking to enter the foreign service, you should be prepared to undergo — in greater or lesser degree — a life of some uncertainty, sacrifice, frustration and even, nowadays, danger. You are likely to spend half or more of your working years abroad, sometimes in inconvenient and even unhappy locales and perhaps with less of the pecuniary rewards to which you think your talents may entitle you. This is, per- haps, putting it bleakly — to be on the safe side; the Cana- dian foreign service, like those of so many other countries, now extends far beyond the attractive capitals of Western

Europe, and you must be prepared to serve elsewhere than in London, Paris, Rome, Geneva, Stockholm, or Madrid. Dozens of other foreign capitals have their attractions too.

When you are posted, one of your first preoccupations will be to rent your home in Ottawa, if you own one, furnished or unfurnished depending on what you expect to find abroad. Furnished housing may be provided you by the mission, especially in capitals where it is hard to find and where the government has "Crown-leased" and furnished some houses or apartments. Or you may be on your own and be housed in a hotel for an initial few days while you seek accommodation, with help from the Mission. Heads of Mission are provided with a furnished official residence. All ranks pay for housing abroad — but only the amount that Treasury calculates they would be paying as rent in Ottawa at that time.

Before going out, "Post Reports" in Ottawa inform you about living conditions, housing, educational and recreational facilities, prices, health and sanitary aspects and information on dozens of other facets of daily living in the area to which you are being posted. Unlike the earlier days when I joined External, there are training programs, pre-posting briefings on subjects related to your area, including terrorism and personal security, and cross- Canada familiarization tours.

In recent years, persons in other government departments in Ottawa are increasingly being given temporary secondments and "lateral transfers" into External, and vice versa. We like to think that we have seeded the public service with some of its best people; certainly a surprising number of External "graduates" hold leadership positions in other government departments.

The lack of opportunities for professional employment of foreign service spouses in some countries can be a problem (although over two dozen countries allow Canadian spouses to work for the duration of a posting). Today, more and more spouses are unwilling to sacrifice careers they pursue in Canada in order to enhance a foreign service person's career abroad. As in other branches of life, but perhaps more markedly in the foreign service, families may experience pressures leading to spousal separation. Also, parents may be unwilling to expose their children to the separation from their families for schooling that service abroad may entail.

How to get on in the foreign service? No matter how lugubrious you may feel, display *panache*, even a touch of *élan*.

No matter how desperately you are awaiting the outcome of some horrendous situation you yourself have brought about, manifest reasonable *insouciance*. Eschew excitability, especially when all hell is breaking loose, and always exude a little *bonhomie* even to enemies or rivals; but flattery of superiors and knee-jerk conformance with their views will get you nowhere. Don't succumb to institutional rigidities and don't hesitate to play the devil's advocate — making it clear, of course, that you *are* playing the devil's advocate.

If you are just dying to get a posting to Kinshasa or Djakarta, study Russian and push for Moscow, or perhaps Rome or Buenos Aires. If you have been a good trooper by sweating it out at three successive hardship posts, don't assume you will next get that dream post, for which you've been waiting, as a just reward; Personnel doesn't have a long memory — except for the mistakes you have made. No matter what they do to your life, display *joie de vivre*, keep your fingers crossed and see what the fates bring you. And remember this adage: what you lose on the swings you may or may not gain on the roundabouts — if you live long enough.

Finally, I don't think it is being "old-fashioned" to assert that, while a foreign service career has many attractions, you and your wife — or you and your husband (there are a growing number of women in the service, whose husbands move with them) — should not contemplate entry unless you are prepared to accept the ethos of service that it entails. A former United States ambassador, Martin Herz, when he was director of studies at Georgetown University's Institute for the Study of Diplomacy, made this point very well some years ago in a symposium on "Diplomacy: the Role of the Wife": "Those who believe that every effort made 'for the government' must be compensated, who look upon every assignment with a calculus of advantages versus disadvantages, who need to 'do their own thing' on their own terms, will miss an entire dimension of the diplomatic life that is different in kind from every other career, except perhaps the military services, because of the discipline that it necessarily requires. A career in diplomacy is simply too demanding and dangerous to be approached in any other spirit. Therefore, unless one can derive some pride from the fact that one is also serving one's country — yes, serving one's country — the inevitable sacrifices and disabilities that are involved will never seem adequately compensated. And this applies as much to husbands as it does to wives."

Index